This book provides helpful answers to questions about psychotherapy supervision that you haven't yet thought to ask. It will help supervisors and supervisees at all levels with its broad and deep perspective on the supervisory relationship, which makes all the difference in the teaching and learning process. Sarnat's experience and practical wisdom are everywhere in this clear, scholarly, and easy-to-read volume.

—**Stephen Seligman, DMH,** Clinical Professor of Psychiatry, Infant-Parent Program, University of California, San Francisco

Joan Sarnat's book is lively, down to earth, and at the same time rich and sophisticated. With the help of moving vignettes, she successfully demonstrates the uniqueness of a relational approach to psychodynamic supervision. She clarifies the value of mutuality in an asymmetrical context, of a nonauthoritarian and nonhierarchical teaching model, and of utilizing experience-near psychodynamic insights not only in the content of supervision but also in its basic structure and style.

—**Emanuel Berman, PhD,** Training Analyst, Israel Psychoanalytic Institute, Haifa

This guide offers a vital perspective, provides highly instructive examples, and will surely become a classic. Sarnat is a master at her craft, and it shows!

—**C. Edward Watkins Jr., PhD,** Professor of Psychology, University of North Texas, Denton

D1570887

Supervision Essentials for

Psychodynamic Psychotherapies

Clinical Supervision
Essentials Series

Supervision Essentials for Psychodynamic Psychotherapies
Joan E. Sarnat

Supervision Essentials for the Integrative Developmental Model
Brian W. McNeill and Cal D. Stoltenberg

CLINICAL SUPERVISION ESSENTIALS

HANNA LEVENSON *and* ARPANA G. INMAN, Series Editors

Supervision Essentials for

Psychodynamic Psychotherapies

Joan E. Sarnat

American Psychological Association • Washington, DC

Published by
American Psychological Association
750 First Street, NE
Washington, DC 20002
www.apa.org

To order
APA Order Department
P.O. Box 92984
Washington, DC 20090-2984
Tel: (800) 374-2721; Direct: (202) 336-5510
Fax: (202) 336-5502; TDD/TTY: (202) 336-6123
Online: www.apa.org/pubs/books
E-mail: order@apa.org

In the U.K., Europe, Africa, and the Middle East, copies may be ordered from
American Psychological Association
3 Henrietta Street
Covent Garden, London
WC2E 8LU England

Typeset in Minion by Circle Graphics, Inc., Columbia, MD

Printer: Maple Press, York, PA
Cover Designer: Mercury Publishing Services, Inc., Rockville, MD

The opinions and statements published are the responsibility of the authors, and such opinions and statements do not necessarily represent the policies of the American Psychological Association.

Library of Congress Cataloging-in-Publication Data

Sarnat, Joan E.
  Supervision essentials for psychodynamic psychotherapies / Joan E. Sarnat. — First edition.
     pages cm
  Includes bibliographical references and index.
  ISBN 978-1-4338-2136-3—ISBN 1-4338-2136-2 1. Psychoanalysis—Study and teaching—Supervision. 2. Psychotherapists—Supervision of. 3. Psychodynamic psychotherapy—Study and teaching—Supervision. I. Title.
  RC502.S27 2016
  616.89'17076—dc23
                              2015019979

British Library Cataloguing-in-Publication Data
A CIP record is available from the British Library.

Printed in the United States of America
First Edition

http://dx.doi.org/10.1037/14802-000

Table of Contents

Foreword to the Clinical Supervision Essentials Series

We are both clinical supervisors. We teach courses on supervision of students who are in training to become therapists. We give workshops on supervision and consult with supervisors about their supervision practices. We write and do research on the topic. To say we eat and breathe supervision might be a little exaggerated, but only slightly. We are fully invested in the field and in helping supervisors provide the most informed and helpful guidance to those learning the profession. We also are committed to helping supervisees/consultees/trainees become better collaborators in the supervisory endeavor by understanding their responsibilities in the supervisory process.

What is supervision? Supervision is critical to the practice of therapy. As stated by Edward Watkins[1] in the *Handbook of Psychotherapy Supervision*, "Without the enterprise of psychotherapy supervision, . . . the practice of psychotherapy would become highly suspect and would or should cease to exist" (p. 603).

Supervision has been defined as

> an intervention provided by a more senior member of a profession to a more junior colleague or colleagues who typically (but not always) are members of that same profession. This relationship
>
> ■ is evaluative and hierarchical,
> ■ extends over time, and

---

[1] Watkins, C. E., Jr. (Ed.) (1997). *Handbook of psychotherapy supervision.* New York, NY: Wiley.

- has the simultaneous purposes of enhancing the professional functioning of the more junior person(s); monitoring the quality of professional services offered to the clients that she, he, or they see; and serving as a gatekeeper for the particular profession the supervisee seeks to enter. (p. 9)[2]

It is now widely acknowledged in the literature that supervision is a "distinct activity" in its own right.[3] One cannot assume that being an excellent therapist generalizes to being an outstanding supervisor. Nor can one imagine that good supervisors can just be "instructed" in how to supervise through purely academic, didactic means.

So how does one become a good supervisor?

Supervision is now recognized as a core competency domain for psychologists[4,5] and other mental health professionals. Guidelines have been created to facilitate the provision of competent supervision across professional groups and internationally (e.g., American Psychological Association,[6] American Association of Marriage and Family Therapy,[7] British Psychological Society,[8,9] Canadian Psychological Association[10]).

---

[2] Bernard, J. M., & Goodyear, R. K. (2014). *Fundamentals of clinical supervision* (5th ed.). Boston, MA: Pearson.

[3] Bernard, J. M., & Goodyear, R. K. (2014). *Fundamentals of clinical supervision* (5th ed.). Boston, MA: Pearson.

[4] Fouad, N., Grus, C. L., Hatcher, R. L., Kaslow, N. J., Hutchings, P. S., Madson, M. B., et al. (2009). Competency benchmarks: A model for understanding and measuring competence in professional psychology across training levels. *Training and Education in Professional Psychology, 3* (4 Suppl.), S5–S26. http://dx.doi.org/10.1037/a0015832

[5] Kaslow, N. J., Rubin, N. J., Bebeau, M. J., Leigh, I. W., Lichtenberg, J. W., Nelson, P. D., et al. (2007). Guiding principles and recommendations for the assessment of competence. *Professional Psychology: Research and Practice, 38,* 441–51. http://dx.doi.org/10.1037/0735-7028.38.4.441

[6] American Psychological Association. (2014). *Guidelines for clinical supervision in health service psychology.* Retrieved from http://www.apa.org/about/policy/guidelines-supervision.pdf

[7] American Association of Marriage and Family Therapy. (2007). *AAMFT approved supervisor designation standards and responsibilities handbook.* Retrieved from http://www.aamft.org/imis15/Documents/Approved_Supervisor_handbook.pdf

[8] British Psychological Society. (2003). *Policy guidelines on supervision in the practice of clinical psychology.* Retrieved from http://www.conatus.co.uk/assets/uploaded/downloads/policy_and_guidelines_on_supervision.pdf

[9] British Psychological Society. (2010). *Professional supervision: Guidelines for practice for educational psychologists.* Retrieved from http://www.ucl.ac.uk/educational-psychology/resources/DECP%20Supervision%20report%20Nov%202010.pdf

[10] Canadian Psychological Association. (2009). *Ethical guidelines for supervision in psychology: Teaching, research, practice and administration.* Retrieved from http://www.cpa.ca/docs/File/Ethics/EthicalGuidelinesSupervisionPsychologyMar2012.pdf

The *Guidelines for Clinical Supervision in Health Service Psychology*[11] are built on several assumptions, specifically that supervision

- requires formal education and training;
- prioritizes the care of the client/patient and the protection of the public;
- focuses on the acquisition of competence by and the professional development of the supervisee;
- requires supervisor competence in the foundational and functional competency domains being supervised;
- is anchored in the current evidence base related to supervision and the competencies being supervised;
- occurs within a respectful and collaborative supervisory relationship that includes facilitative and evaluative components and is established, maintained, and repaired as necessary;
- entails responsibilities on the part of the supervisor and supervisee;
- intentionally infuses and integrates the dimensions of diversity in all aspects of professional practice;
- is influenced by both professional and personal factors, including values, attitudes, beliefs, and interpersonal biases;
- is conducted in adherence to ethical and legal standards;
- uses a developmental and strength-based approach;
- requires reflective practice and self-assessment by the supervisor and supervisee;
- incorporates bidirectional feedback between the supervisor and supervisee;
- includes evaluation of the acquisition of expected competencies by the supervisee;
- serves a gatekeeping function for the profession; and
- is distinct from consultation, personal psychotherapy, and mentoring.

The importance of supervision can be attested to by increased state laws and regulations that certify supervisors and the required multiple supervisory practica and internships that graduate students in all professional programs must complete. Furthermore, research has

---

[11] American Psychological Association. (2014). *Guidelines for clinical supervision in health service psychology.* Retrieved from http://www.apa.org/about/policy/guidelines-supervision.pdf

confirmed[12] the high prevalence of supervisory responsibilities among practitioners—specifically that between 85% and 90% of all therapists eventually become clinical supervisors within the first 15 years of practice.

So now we see the critical importance of good supervision and its high prevalence. We also have guidelines for its competent practice and an impressive list of objectives. But is this enough to become a good supervisor? Not quite. One of the best ways to learn is from highly regarded supervisors—the experts in the field—those who have the procedural knowledge[13] to know what to do, when, and why.

Which leads us to our motivation for creating this series. As we looked around for materials that would help us supervise, teach, and research clinical supervision, we were struck with the lack of a coordinated effort to present the essential models of supervision in both a didactic and experiential form through the lens of expert supervisors. What seemed to be needed was a forum where the experts in the field—those with the knowledge *and* the practice—present the basics of their approaches in a readable, accessible, concise fashion and demonstrate what they do in a real supervisory session. The need, in essence, was for a showcase of best practices.

This series, then, is an attempt to do just that. We considered the major approaches to supervisory practice—those that are based on theoretical orientation and those that are meta-theoretical. We surveyed psychologists, teachers, clinical supervisors, and researchers domestically and internationally working in the area of supervision. We asked them to identify specific models to include and who they would consider to be experts in this area. We also asked this community of colleagues to identify key issues that typically need to be addressed in supervision sessions. Through this consensus building, we came up with a dream team of 11 supervision experts who not only have developed a working model of supervision but also have been in the trenches as clinical supervisors for years.

---

[12] Rønnestad, M. H., Orlinsky, D. E., Parks, B. K., & Davis, J. D. (1997). Supervisors of Psychotherapy: Mapping experience level and supervisory confidence. *European Psychologist, 2,* 191–201.

[13] Schön, D.A. (1987). *Educating the reflective practitioner: Toward a new design for teaching and learning in the professions.* San Francisco, CA: Jossey-Bass.

We asked each expert to write a concise book elucidating her or his approach to supervision. This included highlighting the essential dimensions/key principles, methods/techniques, and structure/process involved, the research evidence for the model, and how common supervisory issues are handled. Furthermore, we asked each author to elucidate the supervisory process by devoting a chapter describing a supervisory session in detail, including transcripts of real sessions, so that the readers could see how the model comes to life in the reality of the supervisory encounter.

In addition to these books, each expert filmed an actual supervisory session with a supervisee so that her or his approach could be demonstrated in practice. APA Books has produced these videos as a series and they are available as DVDs (http://www.apa.org/pubs/videos). Each of these books and videos can be used together or independently, as part of the series or alone, for the reader aspiring to learn how to supervise, for supervisors wishing to deepen their knowledge, for trainees wanting to be better supervisees, for teachers of courses on supervision, and for researchers investigating this pedagogical process.

ABOUT THIS BOOK

In this book, *Supervision Essentials for Psychodynamic Psychotherapies*, Joan Sarnat works from an intersubjective model. This relational context puts the supervisory relationship front and center. The supervisor's goal is to foster an environment in which supervisees feel free to share and bring material into the supervisory relationship that they would otherwise feel too shameful to acknowledge and receive help with emotional issues that are most troubling in their work with patients. In this approach, the supervisory relationship must feel safe enough to allow supervisees to share their authentic experience and yet challenge them enough to stimulate growth and development. Drawing on work from education, cognitive science, and neuroscience, Dr. Sarnat describes a clear framework for developing the supervisee's emotional and relational competencies. Her wealth of clinical experience and the many supervisory vignettes she provides make this a valuable, experience-near book for supervisors and supervisees alike.

We thank you for your interest and hope the books in this series enhance your work in a stimulating and relevant way.

Hanna Levenson and Arpana G. Inman

Acknowledgments

This book would not have come into being without Dr. Hanna Levenson's invitation and her devotion to making this series a reality. Thanks to her, Dr. Arpana Inman, and Ida Audeh for their editorial input. I also want to acknowledge Shari Nacson, for her close and thoughtful reading of my work, and Kristopher Spring, for his copyediting savvy. Dr. Clifton Watkins provided me with an invaluable road map to the latest supervision literature, greatly enriching both my knowledge and the book. Many thanks, too, to my supervisees, who allowed me to make use of our work and who have taught me so much. Finally, deep appreciation to my husband, David Hoffman, for his support of this project and for being willing to share me with it for so many months.

Supervision Essentials for

Psychodynamic Psychotherapies

Introduction

A predoctoral psychology supervisee, Jane,[1] is enmeshed in a struggle with her client, Susie, with whom she has been working for 3 years. Jane cares deeply for Susie but also feels intensely frustrated by her at times. Right now, Jane is preparing to leave the training clinic where she has been seeing Susie to start a clinical internship nearby. Jane has invited Susie to follow her there, but Susie insists that doing so would demand too much of her, and she will not commit to the transfer. She has shut down, become dismissive of the psychotherapy, and is minimizing her feelings of attachment to Jane.

Jane is a thoughtful intern who has a good beginning understanding of how to conduct psychodynamic psychotherapy. She knows "in her head" that Susie is defending herself against feelings of hurt, anger, and vulnerability, feelings that are unbearable given Susie's

[1]The names and identifying information of all supervisees and all patients have been changed to protect their identities.

http://dx.doi.org/10.1037/14802-001
Supervision Essentials for Psychodynamic Psychotherapies, by J. E. Sarnat
Copyright © 2016 by the American Psychological Association.

history of early abandonments and parental neglect and abuse. But, right now, Jane is hurt and angry herself and feels critical of how Susie is behaving. Unwittingly, Jane has gotten caught up in a power struggle with her patient.

As Jane talks about the situation, her supervisor expresses empathy for both Susie's and Jane's plights. The supervisor also makes a number of efforts to help Jane to see and understand what is going on, and to reconnect Jane to the frightened "little Susie," with whom Jane seems to have lost contact. However, the supervisor's efforts seem to be of little use. Jane nods, and expresses agreement with her supervisor's comments in a compliant way, but does not really work with her supervisor's observations. After this goes on for a while, the supervisor begins to feel frustrated, too.[2]

This situation describes my dilemma in working with a supervisee. A portion of the session in which this occurred is transcribed and discussed in chapter 4 of this book.

A RELATIONAL MODEL OF PSYCHODYNAMIC SUPERVISION

Supervisors inevitably struggle with such dilemmas. *Supervision Essentials for Psychodynamic Psychotherapies* is intended to help supervisors to think about—and expand their options for how to work with—such dilemmas. Bringing relational psychoanalytic ideas to bear, Mary Gail Frawley-O'Dea (1997a, 1997b, 1997c, 1998) and I (Sarnat, 1992, 1997, 1998) began, independently, to develop a similar approach to supervising. We then collaborated on fleshing out the model as coauthors in *The Supervisory Relationship* (Frawley-O'Dea & Sarnat, 2001) and have continued to do so in subsequent publications (Beck, Sarnat, & Barenstein, 2008; Burka, Sarnat, & St. John, 2007; Frawley-O'Dea, 2003; Sarnat, 2006, 2008, 2010, 2012, 2014).

This relational model of psychodynamic supervision puts the supervisory relationship front and center in the mind of the supervisor and

---

[2]The full hour appears in the DVD *Relational Psychodynamic Psychotherapy Supervision* (2015), available at http://www.apa.org/pubs/videos/index.aspx.

guides the supervisor toward creating an interpersonal context (Sarnat, 1992) in which it becomes both possible and ethical to work experientially in the here and now of the supervisory relationship. The model offers a framework within which more may be felt and understood about both the supervisory and clinical relationships.

A number of questions may occur to the reader about such a model. How exactly does one create an interpersonal environment where more can be experienced and known than is possible in more didactic, patient-focused, and hierarchical supervisory relationships? Does a supervisor who thinks relationally neglect didactic teaching, the traditional "bread and butter" of supervision? How does the relational supervisor work within boundaries and in a respectful way, while also engaging deeply with the supervisee?[3] This volume explores these questions and more. In so doing, it will, I hope, enlarge the reader's sense of what is possible during the hours spent teaching and learning the art of psychodynamic psychotherapy.

I will provide both theory and evidence for this approach, and will offer numerous vignettes and detailed supervisory process. Through this material, I hope to bring together the best of two different ways of conceiving of the process of supervising psychodynamically oriented treatments. Eizirik (2014), in discussing a collection of articles on psychoanalytic supervision, noted that some of the contributing authors treated supervision as a process of developing a set of skills and abilities that can be clearly defined and monitored—that is, they approached supervision as "psychological science." In contrast, he noted that another group of contributing authors seemed to conceive of supervision as more "art" than science, an art that was based on an ultimately inscrutable process of emotional learning. This second subset of authors, emphasizing "the uniqueness and the peculiar nature of each analytic relation" (p. 643) and the unique process through which each analyst acquired his or her own analytic identity, was opposed to systematizing or quantifying the "mystery" of what transpires in a supervisory relationship. As both a psycho-

---

[3]For purposes of clarity, the supervisor and the patient are given a feminine pronoun, whereas the supervisee is given a masculine pronoun.

analyst and a psychologist, I identify with each of these points of view and think of them as complementary: I think that systematizing-averse psychoanalysts have something to learn from hard-headed psychologists, and empirically oriented psychologists have something to learn from engaged-in-the-mystery psychoanalytic psychotherapists. In this book, I hope to build bridges between these worlds, referring, at times, to competencies, psychological standards and codes, and "hard-headed" research, and at other times exploring, in-depth, the experience of particular supervisory pairs, in an effort to capture what is "unique and peculiar" about a given supervisory relationship.

In the remaining pages of this introduction, I will first provide some historical context for the book as a psychodynamic and specifically *relational* psychodynamic approach to supervising. I will go on to consider the issue of *process consistency* in supervision, looking at the relationship between the treatment approach that is being taught in supervision and the supervisory approach itself. I will then describe my own process of becoming a relationally oriented psychoanalytic supervisor. Finally, I will describe the readership for whom this book was intended, and offer readers a "road map" to the rest of the book.

THE ORIGINS OF PSYCHODYNAMIC SUPERVISION

Psychodynamic psychotherapy, of course, grew out of Sigmund Freud's revolutionary theory and treatment, psychoanalysis. Freud was profoundly progressive in his willingness to grant a voice to his female hysterical patients, who had been silenced and treated with contempt by others. He was also determined to find meaning in their symptoms rather than viewing their symptoms as only pathological. On the other hand, Freud and many of his followers assumed a hierarchical attitude toward their patients that, although typical of that era, was highly problematic.

As Frawley-O'Dea and I noted in *The Supervisory Relationship* (2001), Freud maintained a strongly hierarchical attitude toward his supervisees as well. In the Wednesday night meetings at Freud's home, in which supervision arguably had its inception, Freud was the unquestioned authority:

One participant remembered that "the last and the decisive word was always spoken by Freud himself" (in Gay, 1988, p. 174). Freud did not hesitate to oust "supervisees," including Adler, Jung, Stekel, and Ferenczi, who, despite their brilliant elaborations of psychoanalytic theory and practice, deviated too much from his "canon."

Freud's authoritarian attitude, sadly, was passed along to many of his analytic descendants, an intergenerational transmission that continues to influence some models of psychoanalytic treatment and supervision today. Psychoanalytic institutes are political places. Supervision can be a means for exerting influence over the new generation—a vehicle for shoring up one's own "camp" within psychoanalysis (Berman, 2004). This politicization of supervision may also explain, at least in part, why psychoanalytic supervisory models have persisted in their hierarchical, supervisor-as-expert orientation long after psychoanalytic clinical models had evolved toward viewing the psychotherapist as a more mutual participant.

One of Freud's most brilliant students, Sándor Ferenczi, held a less hierarchical attitude toward his patients and was prescient in his understanding of the analytic relationship as a relationship between participants who are more alike than different. We can imagine that he maintained a similar attitude toward his supervisees, thus serving as an alternative forefather for relational models of psychodynamic supervision. In the tradition of Ferenczi, each member of the supervisory dyad would be understood to be fully human and, therefore, an unconscious contributor to any difficulties that arise in that relationship (Frawley-O'Dea & Sarnat, 2001).

THE DEVELOPMENT OF A RELATIONAL MODEL OF PSYCHODYNAMIC PSYCHOTHERAPY

According to Aron and Starr (2013), almost as soon as psychodynamic psychotherapy emerged as an offshoot of psychoanalysis, psychoanalysis proper began to assault it. Psychoanalysts, especially those within the United States who followed more in the tradition of Freud than of Ferenczi, created a radical dichotomy between psychoanalysis and psychodynamic psychotherapy, treating psychodynamic psychotherapy as "other" and splitting off and projecting into it all that was unwanted from within psychoanalysis. Thus, "suggestion" and any relational factors that helped the patient (vs. the "pure gold" of insight) and the feminine (vs. the male/phallic) were relegated to psychotherapy. Conducted by "nurturant" female social workers, rather than by "scientific" male physicians, psychotherapy was considered a second-rate treatment to be offered to those who could not "tolerate" the challenges of "real" psychoanalysis or afford its cost.

As Aron and Starr (2013) observed, American relational psychoanalysts have pushed back against this polarization of psychoanalysis and psychotherapy, asserting that relationship and insight are *both* of value, as are science and care, and the "feminine" and the "masculine." They believe that choices about how silent versus participatory the psychotherapist should be, about how frequently the patient should be seen, and about whether or not the couch should be used are equally legitimate and should be determined by the specific needs and preferences of the individuals involved and the situation in which they find themselves. They have argued that five-sessions-per-week, on-the-couch treatments are not by definition superior to other forms of psychodynamic treatment, even though more intensive treatments may be necessary for treating some patients. It is this view of psychodynamic psychotherapy that I subscribe to and that serves as the basis for my model of relational psychodynamic supervision.

THE RELATIONSHIP BETWEEN TREATMENT MODEL AND SUPERVISORY MODEL

Falender and Shafranske (2004) consider psychodynamic supervision to be a "clinical model based"[4] form of supervision. This description of psychodynamic supervision assumes that all psychodynamic supervisors teach the same clinical model, and from my point of view this is an oversimplification

---

[4]Bernard and Goodyear (1998) called supervisory models that had been developed as extensions of clinical theory (and that are used to train clinicians to work in that clinical model) "clinical models based" forms of supervision. They differentiated such models of supervision from models that were developed specifically for supervision without ties to any particular clinical theory.

that is misleading in several ways. Beyond the distinctions between Freud and Ferenczi already discussed, many "flavors" of psychoanalytic theory and practice have proliferated. For the purposes of this monograph, it is important to keep in mind the distinction between more classical, one-person, intrapsychic models, such as those employed by Freudian, ego-psychological, and Kleinian clinicians, and the more relational, two-person, intersubjective models, originated by Ferenczi, Winnicott, Bion, and the interpersonalists and more recently employed by the American relational school and authors such as Ogden, Bollas, Ferro, and Civitarese.

If we keep in mind the distinction between relational and nonrelational approaches to both psychodynamic psychotherapy and psychodynamic supervision, it follows that a supervisor can, for example, be teaching an intersubjectively informed model of treatment but supervising in a non-relational way. Such supervisors are *process-inconsistent* in their approach. This matters because process-inconsistent supervision is less pedagogically effective than process-consistent supervision, in which the supervisor not only "talks the talk" but "walks the walk" (Sarnat, 2012).

Process-inconsistent psychodynamic supervision has developed, in my view, because of the conservatism inherent in the apprenticeship model through which supervisors, until recently, have learned to supervise. Without the benefit of specific supervision training, one's manner of supervising is picked up informally—and often without awareness—from one's own supervisors, supervisors doing to their supervisees as was done to them. As a result, a nonrelational approach to psychoanalytic supervision had been passed with impressive fidelity from Freud through the generations of supervisors, even though those same supervisors' clinical models often have evolved substantially.

Limitations of Process-Inconsistent Supervision: An Example

Frawley-O'Dea (1997a) and Hirsch (1997) wrote complementary papers about their experiences as supervisee and supervisor during Frawley-O'Dea's psychoanalytic training. Frawley-O'Dea was struggling in the transference-countertransference with a patient who was a survivor of early childhood sexual abuse. She found the inconsistency between Hirsch's interpersonal clinical orientation and his more classical, hierarchical, didactic supervisory approach to be particularly problematic in her work with this patient. Frawley-O'Dea felt that the difficulties with which she most needed help in supervision could not be accessed through her supervisor's approach, which focused primarily on the patient's verbal material. She came to realize that essential material was being communicated in nonsemantic, affective registers in both the clinical and supervisory relationships and was being enacted between supervisor and supervisee via the parallel process. Hirsch eventually concurred with Frawley-O'Dea that his supervisory approach had insufficiently helped Frawley-O'Dea with these experiences.

Process-Consistent Supervision

In contrast, some supervisors have delineated supervision models that are explicitly based on the clinical approach they are trying to teach. Ekstein and Wallerstein (1972) used ego-psychological principles to teach an ego-psychological form of psychodynamic psychotherapy; Jarmon (1990) used object relations concepts to teach an object-relations–based form of psychotherapy; Ungar and de Ahumada (2001) used a Bionian approach to teach Bionian clinical technique; and Frawley-O'Dea and I have drawn upon relational psychoanalytic principles to create our approach to supervising intersubjectively informed psychodynamic psychotherapy. Process-consistent supervisors teach in a way that is experientially rich and model the approach the supervisee is trying to learn.

HOW I CAME TO A RELATIONAL
MODEL OF SUPERVISION

In 1976, immediately after obtaining my psychology license, I was called upon to supervise trainees in the university clinic in which I was employed. I had received no training in supervision, as was typical for that era. However, a trip to the psychology library turned up Ekstein and Wallerstein's (1972) book. I was impressed by the power of their process-consistent and supervisee-focused model of supervision, which offered supervisees help with their own conflicts and resistances as these manifested in the supervisory and clinical relationships. This was exactly the kind of help I had yearned for in my own training.

Although some of the clinical faculty at the University of Michigan had come from The Menninger Clinic, where Ekstein and Wallerstein had developed their supervisory model, they tended to work in supervision in a patient-focused, didactic, nonexperiential, and process-inconsistent manner. My supervisors focused sparingly on the anxieties and resistances that emerged in my work and did not attend to what was being lived out in the supervisory relationship itself. Even Edward Bordin, who developed the concept of the supervisory alliance in his writing (1983), shied away from focusing directly on our relationship and the conflicts that emerged in it and in my relationships with my patients. Although I was engaged in a helpful psychodynamic psychotherapy, my therapist could not provide the specific help with how my conflicts emerged with my patients that a supervisor might have.

When, a few years later, I had an opportunity to supervise a group of graduate students in a university department of clinical psychology, I checked in with my new colleagues about how they supervised. There, too, I found myself alone in my admiration for Ekstein and Wallerstein's experiential, supervisee-focused, and process-consistent approach to supervising. Several colleagues let me know that they were wary of Ekstein and Wallerstein's model because they found that when they focused on their supervisees' psychologies, supervisee anxiety escalated to unmanageable levels, interfering with teaching and learning.

This was not my experience as a supervisor. I was able to address my supervisees' psychologies without much difficulty and found my supervisees to be eager for the help I was offering. Why? Eventually, I concluded that my colleagues must have run into difficulty because they were trying to address their supervisees' psychologies from a position of "objectivity,"[5] while I was open with my supervisees in exploring how my own conflicts

---

[5]Ekstein and Wallerstein, writing before the advent of the relational turn in psychoanalysis, also assumed supervisor objectivity. See Sarnat (1992) and Frawley-O'Dea and Sarnat (2001).

and resistances contributed to difficulties in the supervisory process. I believe that my stance created an interpersonal context in which it was safer for supervisees to acknowledge their conflicts and resistances (Sarnat, 1992).

When I looked back later on how I differed from my colleagues, I realized that I had been influenced by larger cultural (countercultural) forces. I had been affected, first, by the "encounter group" movement. When I was a graduate student, I received training from an extracurricular organization that taught graduate students such as myself to run groups for undergraduates, based on an amalgam of National Training Laboratory and Tavistock group models. My experience as a leader of these groups (which had a strongly egalitarian tone) helped me to see that I was as much affected by unconscious conflicts as were members of my groups. I learned this lesson simultaneously with my immersion in ego-psychological training in graduate school, where it was assumed that (well-analyzed) therapists and supervisors were capable of keeping their conflicts out of their professional relationships.

A few years later, I was further affected by a transformation in psychoanalytic theory itself. Relational psychoanalysis began to emerge in the meetings of the newly formed Division of Psychoanalysis (Division 39) of The American Psychological Association. I found this fresh perspective on psychoanalysis both exciting and helpful in formulating what I was already doing as a supervisor and a clinician but had been unable to articulate coherently. My efforts to sort all of this out for myself led me to write my first paper arguing for a relational approach to psychodynamic supervision (Sarnat, 1992).

Over time, more fully elaborated relational and intersubjective conceptualizations of psychodynamic supervision began to emerge in the literature. My book with Frawley-O'Dea (2001) contributed to this process of theory building.

THE AUDIENCE FOR THIS BOOK

Psychodynamic and psychoanalytic supervisors who want to deepen their knowledge of the art of supervision, as well as those who aspire to become supervisors, are the primary intended audience for this book. Supervisees who want to approach supervision with a clearer sense of the full range of possibilities for how one may work in supervision will also find the book useful.

In addition, this book may be of interest to supervisors and supervisees who do not specifically identify as psychodynamic. All supervisors face the challenge of establishing and maintaining growth-promoting relationships with their supervisees and, in turn, teaching their supervisees how to establish and maintain growth-promoting relationships with their patients. All supervisors should become aware of the power of experiential learning and how to create a supervisory situation in which this kind of learning is possible and ethical. Thus, many of the insights offered in this book may be useful to supervisors who teach a variety of models of psychotherapy, including cognitive behavioral therapy (CBT), existential, family therapy, and others, as well as psychoanalysis proper. Similarly, it may be of use to supervisees who are being trained in those clinical models.

AN OVERVIEW OF THE CONTENT OF THIS BOOK

In chapter 1, I define three essential dimensions of a relational model of psychodynamic supervision, using those dimensions to differentiate the model from what I call "classical model" supervision. First is the nature of the supervisor's view of her knowledge and authority, which is a more egalitarian and perspectival view than is found in a classical model. Second is the range of material taken up in supervision, which is much broader than in a classical approach. Third is the supervisor's mode of participation, which goes beyond the classically didactic to include experiential and "quasitherapeutic" interventions, always used in the service of the educational task.

In chapter 2, we take a look at the empirical evidence supporting the effectiveness of a relational approach to psychodynamic supervision. Drawing on the limited supervision research literature, as well as research literature from psychotherapy, education, cognitive science, and neuroscience, I present evidence that suggests that essential aspects of the relational model are good pedagogy. In particular, research findings support the model's emphasis on attending to the supervisory relationship as a means of enhancing emotional and relational competencies in a psychodynamic psychotherapist.

Having provided the theoretical and empirical basis for the relational model of psychodynamic supervision, I go on, in chapter 3, to describe some of the model's specific methods. This chapter discusses how to individualize supervision to fit the learning needs of the supervisee, how to select the format in which material will be presented in supervision, and how to approach evaluation and documentation. Finally, I present in some detail my thoughts about how to facilitate supervisee development in case conference.

Chapters 1, 2, and 3 prepare the reader for chapter 4, which is an excerpt from a transcript of my actual supervisory work. This session, which I referred to at the beginning of this chapter, makes explicit my process as I begin to recognize that my efforts to "teach" my supervisee are proving ineffective. I describe my thinking as I stop trying to "impart wisdom" to her and begin to work with her in the here and now.

The next three chapters address issues that all supervisors confront. In these chapters, I explain what the values and techniques of a relational model of psychodynamic supervision can contribute to a supervisor's way of working with each of those issues.

Chapter 5 explores working with supervisee "difficulties." I sketch a continuum from "normative" difficulties, a form of regression in the service of growth and learning; to "moderate" difficulties, which require significant work in the here and now of the supervisory relationship; to "serious" difficulties, which may not be amenable to supervisory work and are far more problematic for both supervisor and supervisee. I offer examples of how I work with supervisees who are at various points along that continuum.

In chapter 6, the issue is working with difference. Here I draw upon the relational psychoanalytic literature to suggest how to work with these challenging issues in both the supervisory and clinical dyads. I also show how a relational approach is well-suited to developing supervisor awareness of her own participation in destructive cultural assumptions; how the model facilitates negotiation of areas of cultural disagreement; and how it supports the supervisor in working through disturbing feelings that emerge when issues of difference come into the supervisory or clinical conversation.

In chapter 7, I consider working with legal/ethical issues. I suggest several ways in which a relational perspective encourages ethical supervisor conduct, in particular, how the model's view of the supervisor's authority supports self-monitoring and counters supervisor arrogance. I also explore legal/ethical areas that require special attention when a supervisor is working relationally—the most important of which is respectful maintenance of the teach–treat boundary.

I conclude, in chapter 8, by imagining future directions for psychodynamic supervision. I suggest that working through supervisors' resistances to the relational model is one important goal, as is opening supervisors' minds to innovative skill development and technological approaches. I emphasize the importance of supervision training. I recommend increasing the availability of consultation (that is, supervision of supervision) to supervisors so that they may be helped to look at their unconscious participation in the supervisory process and be protected from burnout. Finally, I propose some ideas for future research on supervision.

In an appendix, I have provided an annotated list of readings for those who would like to further delve into the literature on relational psychodynamic supervision. Here, supervisors as well as supervisees, and psychotherapists as well as psychoanalysts, should find additional material relevant to their specific interests.

By presenting and demonstrating this relational model of psychodynamic supervision, I hope to help the reader discover how to better facilitate the development of emotionally available, skillful, and self-reflective psychodynamic psychotherapists. Join me in exploring the enigmatic art of helping psychotherapists to grow.

1

Essential Dimensions

In this chapter, I lay out the essential components of a relational model of psychodynamic supervision, starting with three key definitions. According to the definition of *supervision* that the editors of this series have provided in their Foreword to this book, it is an evaluative, gate-keeping activity. In this way, it is different from what I call *consultation*, which I define as an activity that takes place between two licensed professionals when one voluntarily seeks clinical help from the other. Although this book focuses specifically on the activity of supervision, most of its principles apply equally well to consultative relationships. What defines a *relational model of psychodynamic supervision*? It is a model of supervision that is primarily, but not exclusively, utilized to supervise psychodynamic or psychoanalytic treatments, and in which relational psychoanalytic concepts inform the supervisor's approach to the supervisory relationship.

http://dx.doi.org/10.1037/14802-002
Supervision Essentials for Psychodynamic Psychotherapies, by J. E. Sarnat
Copyright © 2016 by the American Psychological Association.

In what follows, I further define this model in terms of three dimensions: Dimension 1, the supervisor's view of her authority; Dimension 2, the nature of the material that is discussed in supervision; and Dimension 3, the supervisor's mode of participation (Frawley-O'Dea & Sarnat, 2001). In describing Dimension 1, I draw upon two papers written by psychoanalytic supervisors, one working from a "classical" model of psychoanalytic supervision and the other working from a relational model. The classical model paper serves as a kind of foil for the relational model paper, bringing the differences in exercise of authority into relief. In explaining Dimension 2, I use two examples of relational supervisory work to demonstrate how the model invites a deepening and broadening of the supervisor's way of thinking and working. In describing Dimension 3, I begin with a vignette that shows the limitations inherent in the classical model and again contrast that approach with a vignette from a relational model supervisor. Next, I present an extended vignette that brings all three dimensions together. The chapter ends with some reflections on the teach–treat boundary.

DIMENSION 1: THE SUPERVISOR'S VIEW OF HER AUTHORITY

To highlight what is distinctive about the relational model's view of authority, we contrast it to a nonrelational or "classical" model of psychodynamic supervision (Frawley-O'Dea & Sarnat, 2001). Two psychoanalyst supervisors who worked from these contrasting models were asked by *Psychoanalytic Dialogues* to describe how they would supervise the same two psychoanalytic candidates, based on written case reports submitted by those candidates. I draw here upon a previous discussion of their papers (Sarnat, 2006).

Bergmann (2003), who worked in a classical way, assumed himself to be in a position of unquestioned expertise and authority in his relationship to his supervisee. He began his essay by providing a detailed description of his clinical model, seeing transmission of his ideas about theory and technique as the primary supervisory task. In discussing Bergmann's case material, Margaret Black (2003) commented: "He seeks, when possible, to build on the candidate's thinking, inviting her to speculate and discuss ideas that may be newly formulated. But he also supplies his own crystal clear vision of analytic function and *expects it to take precedence*" (pp. 368–369, italics added). Bergmann sees the supervisor as someone who is authoritative but not unsympathetic, observing that his approach demands from the supervisor "freedom from excessive fear of injuring the supervisee's self-esteem, but also not inflicting a needless damage on this self-esteem" (p. 332). Bergmann does not see the pedagogical value of exploring his supervisee's point of view. He does not encourage his supervisees to raise differences for discussion, and they are therefore left to wrestle internally with any disagreements that arise.

A contrasting, relational view of the supervisor's authority is expressed in Frawley-O'Dea's (2003) essay. She provides no list of theoretical and technical principles to be conveyed to the reader or to her supervisees. Instead, she wants to know which theoretical concepts and technical approaches *this* supervisee finds useful in thinking about *this* patient. Privileging process over content, she considers the meaning of agreement or disagreement between supervisor and supervisee more important than the theoretical conceptualizations themselves. Frawley-O'Dea (2003) put it this way:

> The supervisory dyad can pause not only to consider the applicability of differing, even competing, conceptualizations but also to examine mutually the process occurring between supervisor and supervisee. Who is influencing whom in a way that leads the supervisee apparently to relinquish her own mind? Is this a dynamic signifying a transference-countertransference constellation particular to the supervision, or does it have parallel meaning for the supervised treatment? (p. 359)

The relational supervisor sees herself as an embedded participant rather than as an objective expert. Authority is shared by the supervisory couple, although a knowledge and experience gradient is understood to exist between them.

In our work (Frawley-O'Dea & Sarnat, 2001; Sarnat, 2006, 2012), we have drawn upon Aron's (1996) clinical concept of "mutuality in the context of asymmetry" to clarify the relational view of the supervisor's authority. This concept posits that basic asymmetries must exist in all supervisory dyads: The supervisor holds responsibility for the frame, that is, setting up the specifics of when and where the supervision will occur, and for maintaining a focus on the supervisory task, for evaluation, and for ethical practice. However, both parties are understood to bring their subjectivities to the work and to participate mutually in unconscious resistance and enactment, that is, the acting out of material that is too painful to be consciously known. Each brings different kinds of knowledge—the supervisee knows the patient firsthand, whereas the supervisor presumably has more experience as a psychotherapist—and a different perspective on events in the clinical and supervisory relationships. Rather than only deriving power from her role, knowledge, and expertise, the supervisor relies on the supervisee to authorize her as a source of influence based on the trust that develops between them (Slavin, 1998). The supervisor positions herself to respond to the emerging supervisory process, a process that often surprises and sometimes stymies her. She further derives her authority from her capacity to work with that process (and her capacity to seek help in working with it when necessary).

DIMENSION 2: THE NATURE OF THE MATERIAL DISCUSSED IN SUPERVISION

Focusing on the Relationship

The relational perspective expands the supervisor's focus beyond the patient and technique to include the supervisory relationship. Bergmann (2003), with his classical model approach, focuses narrowly on the patient's psychology, as described in the case report, and on his view of technique. It is apparent that he does not consider working with the supervisory relationship to be of pedagogical value. In contrast, Frawley-O'Dea (2003) comments that, on the basis of written case reports she could not imagine how she would supervise the two candidates: She was not in relationship with them.

In the relational model of psychodynamic supervision, the focus on working in the supervisory relationship extends far beyond repairing ruptures in the supervisory alliance. The relational supervisor attends to dynamics that originate in the supervisory relationship, as well as resonances between the supervised clinical relationship and the supervisory relationship. By working with these dynamics, the supervisor demonstrates to her supervisee how to work with similar dynamics in the therapeutic relationship, offering the supervisee a direct experience of how to do so.

Focusing on Nonsemantic Material in the Supervisory Relationship

The relational supervisor pays attention to feelings, somatic experiences, and enactments that arise in the supervisory session, realizing that this nonsemantic material provides information about the clinical relationship that may not be accessed in any other way. This kind of material is sometimes neglected in classical approaches. Neuropsychology (Schore, 2011), infant observation (Lachmann, 2001), cognitive science (Binder, 1999), and contemporary thinking about trauma and primitive states (Gurevich, 2008) have all emphasized the need for psychotherapists to learn to work with nonsemantic states (Vivona, 2006). Concepts such as the "unthought known" (Bollas, 1987), "unformulated experience" (Stern, 1997), and dissociated self-states that are expressed via enactments (Davies & Frawley, 1994) have become common in contemporary psychodynamic psychotherapeutic parlance, so supervisors must learn how to teach supervisees to work with such material. The relational model facilitates the process of doing so (Sarnat, 2012).

To illustrate how relational psychodynamic supervision works with nonsemantic material as it enters the supervisory relationship, I offer two vignettes. In the first (Sarnat, 2014), supervisee and supervisor struggle with a dissociative state. In the second (Sarnat, 1992), supervisor and supervisee become caught up in an enactment.

Vignette 1: Working With Dissociation

A psychoanalytic candidate presented to me her work with a patient who had a history of severe early trauma. Initially, the supervision and the analysis went well. However, about 2 years in, the analytic hours became flat and repetitive. It was hard to make anything of the verbal content of the hours. The supervisory interaction also felt empty and pointless. I realized that my supervisee and I had to find a way to work with the deadness that had overtaken us both, but I couldn't figure out how to do it.

Eventually I brought the supervisory situation to my peer consultation group. As I told them about the situation, I became aware that I was feeling as overwhelmed by despair as my supervisee and her patient were. As we explored this parallel process, we realized that each member of the supervisory triad had her particular vulnerability to being overtaken by these feelings. I had been able to help my supervisee work with the patient's vulnerabilities and with her own vulnerabilities but needed my colleagues' help to work with a related vulnerability that had been touched in me: feelings of doubt in myself as a supervisor of an analysis. I was particularly gripped by those feelings because this was the first psychoanalytic case that I had supervised. I talked about this with my colleagues, and they expressed confidence in my capacity to supervise the case. I was especially relieved to know that they considered my asking for help to be a sign of strength rather than an expression of my not being ready to supervise an analysis. Something began to shift in me; I began to feel more like myself.

I returned to my supervisee and spoke with her about what I had experienced in consultation. When I let her know that I needed help just as she did, her feelings of failure and shame abated. We then began to work our way out of the parallel impasses that had developed in our relationship and in the supervised analysis. As our supervisory relationship came back to life, my supervisee found herself able to be with her patient in a different way, and the treatment came back to life as well.

Vignette 2: Working With Enactment

Early in my career as a supervisor (Sarnat, 1992), I worked with an advanced doctoral student who, although gifted in many ways, had difficulty appropriately asserting herself with her patients. We could not ignore this because several of these patients were not paying their fees. My initial approach with my supervisee was similar to that of Ekstein and Wallerstein (1972): I focused on her "learning problem," her defensive style. I tried to clarify with her how her inhibition operated and offered her examples of how she might talk more assertively to her patients, "teaching" from a position of objective expertise. Although taking this approach was not helping her (her patients were getting worse), for a while I persisted, not knowing what else to do.

I eventually became aware that in continuing to advise my supervisee about what she should do differently I was *enacting* something with her. That is, I was living out a scenario with her because something inside of me—my unprocessed internalized relationship with an authoritarian object—was too painful for me to be aware of. She, in turn, was carrying my authoritarian manner into her relationships with her patients, via the parallel process. That is, she was unconsciously identifying with, and possibly parodying, my way of relating. Naturally, when my supervisee did this, trouble with her patients ensued.

Just as I was becoming aware of my participation in this enactment, my supervisee found the courage to confront me. I believe that the timing was not coincidental but that her preconscious awareness that something had shifted in me freed her to speak. My previously soft-spoken supervisee now expressed to me her fury about how destructive my supervisory approach was to her. I managed to tolerate her outburst nondefensively. Somewhat to my surprise, I found that my openness to her anger helped her in a way that my disengaged advice had not. After this interchange, which had little to do with the specifics of what was being said in the clinical sessions but everything to do with the states of mind that were flowing up and down the supervisory triad, my supervisee was better able to access her healthy aggression in her work, and her relationships with her patients improved.

Discussion

Both of these vignettes illustrate how one may facilitate a supervisee's capacity to work with hard-to-access nonsemantic elements in the therapeutic relationship by attending to and working with related elements in the supervisory relationship. By broadening the scope of what supervisor and supervisee can do together, the relational model addresses the unsymbolized states that are understood in contemporary treatment models to be essential to address to facilitate change.

DIMENSION 3: THE SUPERVISOR'S MODE OF PARTICIPATION—USING ONE'S CLINICAL EXPERTISE IN SUPERVISION

A psychoanalytic supervisor who works in a classical way assumes that teaching excludes "treating" the supervisee, as though those activities can be kept completely separate. If a supervisee begins to express strong feelings toward the supervisor, for example, she likely will minimize those feelings or ask that the supervisee take them to his psychotherapist or analyst. When intense and disruptive feelings toward the patient come up, she may do the same. Unfortunately, not all supervisees are in treatment, and even those who are can't always use their treatment to focus on the issue the supervisor feels should be addressed. (See chap. 7 in *The Supervisory Relationship* [Frawley-O'Dea & Sarnat, 2001] for an extensive discussion of this issue.)

In contrast, from a relational perspective, teaching and "treating" are viewed as part of a complex, integrated process. The emergence of strong feelings in supervision is therefore understood to provide pedagogical opportunities. A relational supervisor draws upon her clinical expertise in working with such feelings, although she does not go further into the supervisee's personal material than the work at hand requires, and keeps the supervisory task, as opposed to a more general treatment task, in the forefront. Even exploring a supervisee's transference toward his supervisor can become an integral part of the educational process, if it is handled judiciously;[1] neglecting to do so can undermine supervisee learning. The following vignette illustrates.

---

[1]See the end of this chapter and also chapter 7 for more on managing the teach–treat boundary.

Vignette: A Classical Supervisor Declines
to Explore a Negative Transference

Dewald (1987) unwittingly provided an example of what may be sacrificed if a supervisor is unwilling to explore negative feelings in the supervisory relationship. In my discussion of this example, I draw upon Frawley-O'Dea and Sarnat (2001, pp. 111–112).

Dewald published a book of transcripts of his supervision of a gifted psychoanalytic candidate, Dr. Dick, and his commentaries on those transcripts. A picture emerged of a very straightforward, classical supervision that proceeded smoothly. However, when Dewald invited Dr. Dick to write a chapter expressing her point of view on the supervision, she mentioned an experience that was at odds with Dewald's narrative. She said she had been taken aback by the emergence of negative feelings toward Dewald during an hour early in the supervision. Disturbed that she could not reconcile these feelings with her predominantly positive—even idealized—experience of Dewald, she raised these feelings with Dewald. Dewald framed her feelings as an identification with her patient's negative transference, and moved on, neglecting the meaning of Dr. Dick's feelings for the supervisory relationship itself. Dr. Dick got the message that such feelings did not belong in supervision. After that single effort to talk about them, her negative feelings never came to mind again when she was in Dewald's presence.

Because these feelings remained unaddressed in her relationship with Dewald, Dr. Dick felt that her work in supervision and her work with her patient were compromised. She could not trust Dewald's evaluation of her because she knew she was hiding much of her true self from him. She was unable to challenge Dewald's formulations when they felt wrong to her because she was afraid that Dewald did not want to hear her negative feelings. Most important, while her "false self" (Eckler-Hart, 1987) remained unaddressed in her relationship with Dewald, she was unable to work with her patient's false-self transference.

I imagine that Dewald, writing in 1987 from within the ego-psychologically–oriented community of the American Psychoanalytic Association, felt that inviting Dr. Dick to explore her negative transference would transgress the teach–treat boundary. He probably did not have a sense of how one could work with such feelings appropriately while remaining true to the supervisory task—or that failing to do so could hold back the supervised analysis.

Vignette: A Relational Supervisor Works With a Supervisee's Transferential Feelings

In contrast to the classical model supervisor, the relational supervisor feels empowered to bring her clinical expertise into the supervisory relationship, using it explicitly in the service of the educational task. In previous work, I described how I used my clinical expertise while working with Lisa (Sarnat, 2010). I provided Lisa with emotional containment and worked with the intense affective states that she brought to me, including self-attack, fears of my criticism, and her projections onto me of judgmental parental figures. Here is an excerpt from my description of a session in which we worked with her intense anxiety about her capacities as a psychotherapist. Early in the supervisory hour she told me she had been suffering acutely since our last meeting, worrying about her ability to work psychodynamically. She also mentioned earlier in the session that her parents didn't like it when she got "too emotional."

> [I asked Lisa whether she had] thought of calling me during this difficult week? Lisa said that she had wanted to, but thought I might be annoyed with her for "overreacting." "Like your parents?" I asked with a smile, and she agreed with a laugh. She seemed relieved, and commented as she left the supervisory meeting that actually she didn't think she was doing so badly in her hours, despite her anxiety. (p. 22)

In this session, I declined, beyond this single comment, to further address Lisa's family history, as I might have with a patient, even though she invited me to do so. Instead, I kept our focus on the here-and-now impediments to our supervisory relationship—that is, her projection onto me of the parents who would criticize her for letting them know she was upset—and on what was pertinent specifically to her development as a clinician. I believe Lisa learned something from this inter-action about her unconscious assumptions about how people whom she depends on will respond to her needs. In so doing, she also learned something about how to work with her patients' emotional needs, an essential element of her development as a psychodynamic psychotherapist. Anxiety about whether one is transgressing the teach–treat boundary can inhibit supervisors from offering to their supervisees this kind of help, help that, in my experience, supervisees like Lisa welcome.[2]

A RELATIONAL VIGNETTE ILLUSTRATING THE THREE DIMENSIONS

When a supervisor holds her own authority yet recognizes her areas of vulnerability; when she enlarges the scope of the material to which she attends in supervision to include nonsemantic experiences and feelings of the supervisee and supervisor toward one another; and when she judiciously brings to bear her clinical skills to further the supervisory task and facilitate supervisee development, profound experiences of supervisee growth and clinical progress become possible. An extended vignette illustrates how these various dimensions of the relational model of psychodynamic supervision came together in my work with a candidate who was struggling with issues of idealization and devaluation in her effort to claim her identity as a psychoanalyst.

I supervised Kathy on her analytic work with Mrs. H. Kathy initially thought the analysis would be relatively straightforward. As the treatment deepened, however, the four weekly sessions with Mrs. H became virtually unbearable for Kathy. Mrs. H began to sleep for extended portions of every hour. Kathy felt paralyzed, feeling that it would be "unanalytic" to wake her patient and that she couldn't talk to Mrs. H about the dilemma because she never seemed to be awake long enough to do so. Meanwhile, Mrs. H was

---

[2] See chapter 5 for guidelines for working with supervisees who are having difficulties and yet are uncomfortable engaging in this way.

engaging in increasingly risky outside-of-session behavior, which terrified Kathy. Kathy described this phase of the analysis in her case write-up:[3]

> I felt as if I had foreknowledge of an impending death, and I further imagined feeling I had stood by and done nothing. . . . I felt gagged, awash in a feeling of accumulated rage. . . . I wanted to rid myself of my feelings of guilt, incompetence, and futility by ending the analysis before she did. . . . In supervision I also felt disorganized and ashamed. How could I, despite many hours of supervision, fail to describe to Mrs. H the multiple ways that terror and passive submission were being evoked in her and enacted between us?

I tried many ways to help Kathy break out of her silence, but my efforts got us nowhere. Kathy became increasingly distraught. As she put it

> The same confusion and desperation that was in the analytic field with Mrs. H. began affecting my relationship with my supervisor. I wondered how my "easy case" had turned into this nightmare, yet I could not get free of my own deadly countertransference sleep to wake my patient up (literally and figuratively) and my supervisor could not wake me.

Kathy was unable to use what I offered, and I was unable to provide what she could use. However, I realized that primitive states of mind were paralleling into our relationship from the analytic relationship, even though I couldn't seem to find an effective way of addressing them with Kathy. Fortunately, she sought help from a seminar leader. He suggested that she say to Mrs. H: "What can I do if you do fall asleep? Can I clap my hands loudly? Can I insist you walk around the office with me?" This recommendation broke into Kathy's paralysis and provided her with permission to act.

In our next supervisory hour, Kathy told me about her experience in the seminar but did so warily, concerned that I might feel wounded by the fact that she had gotten needed help from someone other than

---

[3] I am grateful to "Kathy" for allowing me to use excerpts from her case write-up, as well for her permission to describe our work together.

me. I did, in fact, have some feelings of failure and competitiveness, but I felt comfortable enough with those feelings that I did not act them out in our supervisory session. I acknowledged to her that she had needed help that I had been unable to provide. I also told her that I was glad that she had found the help she needed and expressed a wish to understand more about the impact of the seminar leader's suggestion on her. As we discussed her experience, I built on the seminar leader's suggestion, using it to think freshly and helpfully about what might have been going on between Kathy and her patient.

Kathy entered the next analytic session feeling less ashamed and more confident. (Feelings of shame and failure were a central concern of the patient.) The combination of the seminar leader's suggestion and our conversation in supervision had broken through Kathy's paralysis and feelings of hopelessness. Soon the patient began to improve as well, staying awake and making significant changes in her mood and her daily life.

In her case write-up, Kathy described the impact of my response when she told me about her seminar leader's suggestion:

> When Dr. Sarnat amplified the helpfulness of my seminar leader's intervention, she helped to free me from living in a world where there is only one good object and the rest are bad. And, when she framed her own work with me as "not previously helpful enough," she modeled repair between separate subjects and tolerating feelings of failure. I did not need to take care of Dr. Sarnat by mirroring her goodness (and taking in the bad feelings), but rather, I could benefit from the comfort of a needed other who could speak to her limits and who welcomed my negative feelings toward her. This process represented a movement away from an entrapping fusion with an idealized authority and demonstrated living in a world where painful realities could be spoken of without destruction. Having my supervisor metabolize these difficult feelings resonated in the treatment.

I had acted from a relational understanding of my authority, acknowledging my limitations and the mutuality of our relationship. I believe that my doing so allowed Kathy to better tolerate her own sense of failure in her work with her patient and helped her to modify her idealized image of what a psychoanalyst should be. This was an image that had tormented her since the beginning of her training and had been impeding her analytic development. She now began to feel that being herself was enough and that taking responsibility for her limitations as a helper, without collapsing or retaliating, as I had done, was therapeutic in itself—perfection not required.

Just as relational model supervisors discourage supervisees from pretending to false competencies, we refrain from assuming false expertise ourselves. When we acknowledge our limitations as supervisors, we model for our supervisees accepting and working with their own limitations as clinicians.

The three essential dimensions of a relational model of supervision— the supervisor's view of her authority (as limited), the kind of material worked with in supervision (the supervisory relationship and nonsemantic material), and the supervisor's use of her clinical expertise (for containing countertransference and remaining nondefensive on behalf of the supervisee's development [tolerating de-idealization])—are demonstrated by this example. Kathy's decision to foreground this supervisory experience in her case write-up seems to me to indicate that, in her mind—as well as in mine— the work we were doing, although arguably "therapeutic" in nature, had not transgressed the teach–treat boundary.

CONCLUSION

A relational model supervisor differs from a classical model supervisor in several important ways: in the way she holds her authority; in the material the supervisor feels is legitimate to work with; and in the supervisor's mode of intervention, especially her understanding that working with feelings toward the supervisor and working in the supervisory relationship can be appropriate and necessary supervisory activities. In the relational model, the supervisory relationship is understood to be more than just a carrier of knowledge and medium for collaboration; it is a formidable vehicle for growth and development. A supervisor's awareness of the power of this relationship and willingness to think about and talk with the supervisee about what is going on in the relationship allow more to be known, expressed, and experienced than in supervisions that are only didactic and patient-focused.

The expansion of the supervisor's role in this model naturally brings up the "teach–treat" controversy: To what degree is it legitimate for the supervisor to "treat" the supervisee in order to train him (DeBell, 1981; Sarnat, 1992)? This question has received a variety of answers in the course of the history of psychoanalysis. The Budapest Model of psychoanalytic training, developed at the institute to which Ferenczi belonged, saw "treating" the candidate as essential to his training and so located the candidate's first supervision within his personal analysis (Szönyi, 2014). The reasoning was that no one could be better positioned than the candidate's analyst to help a candidate with the conflicts that conducting analysis stirred up in him. However, this arrangement also created complications, especially the fact that a supervisor must evaluate the candidate in addition to helping him develop. Because of these complications, most psychoanalytic institutes rejected the Budapest Model and made supervision an educational activity that was completely separate from the candidate's personal analysis.

One way of thinking about the relational model, then, is that it seeks to reclaim some of what was lost when institutes drew a bright line between personal analysis and supervision: Rather than bring supervision into the personal analysis, the relational model allows the supervisor to adopt some of the functions of the personal analyst for the purpose of training the supervisee. The relational supervisor assumes these functions with care, mindful that her use of her clinical expertise must be bounded by the limits of the educational task and the availability for such work of this particular supervisee. The dyad can then arrive at an individualized construction of the teach–treat boundary that feels safe, right, and useful to both. Chapter 3 addresses the importance of the supervisee authorizing such work and how to negotiate undertaking it. Chapter 7 discusses the ethical issues surrounding the teach–treat boundary.

Having elaborated the essential dimensions of the relational model, I consider next, in chapter 2, the evidence for the effectiveness of the model. As I reviewed the literature, I was delighted to discover that the evidence strongly supports the effectiveness of the relational psychodynamic approach to teaching the art of psychodynamic psychotherapy.

2

Evidence for the Effectiveness of a Relational Model of Psychodynamic Supervision

In this chapter, I present evidence for the effectiveness of the relational model of psychodynamic supervision. As someone who arrived at this approach to supervising intuitively, I have been surprised and heartened to discover how much empirical data actually support the model. In this chapter I will show that although process and outcome research on psychoanalytic supervision per se is limited (Watkins, 2013), research from that literature, when combined with the counseling psychology supervision literature and the related fields of psychotherapy, education, cognitive psychology, and neuroscience, provides convincing evidence for the pedagogical effectiveness of this affectively rich, experiential, relationship-focused mode of supervision.

http://dx.doi.org/10.1037/14802-003
Supervision Essentials for Psychodynamic Psychotherapies, by J. E. Sarnat
Copyright © 2016 by the American Psychological Association.

THE PSYCHOANALYTIC SUPERVISION RESEARCH LITERATURE

Doehrman (1976) conducted an early and influential study that highlighted the power of the supervisory relationship to derail or enhance the supervised treatment. She interviewed psychoanalytic psychotherapy trainees and their supervisors and found that supervisees carried the difficulties that they were experiencing with their patients into their relationships with their supervisors (parallel process). She also found that not until the supervisor had worked through the difficulty that the supervisee had introduced and become able to interact differently with the supervisee could the supervisee make progress with the patient. Because the study was published before relational psychoanalytic theory had been developed, the profound implications of these early findings were not integrated into supervision theory for a number of years.

More recently, Szecsödy (1990, 2013) conducted a descriptive, hypothesis-generating study to investigate the learning process in psychoanalytic supervision. He analyzed supervision tapes of supervisors who worked with supervisees over a period of months. He concluded that supervisees learned most when the information provided by the supervisor was adapted to the supervisee's immediate needs. He observed, however, that the supervisors in his study often seemed misguidedly "to act according to an assumption that giving information was always useful and/or optimal and was without exception utilizable by the trainee" (p. 221). In addition, he found that supervisee difficulties in supervision reliably turned out to be connected to their difficulties with patients. This study suggests that a classical, didactic method of supervising (providing information whether or not it was relevant to the supervisee's process) was common among supervisors and ineffective.

Nagell, Steinmetzer, Fissabre, and Spilski (2014), in a questionnaire-based study, looked at supervision process and its impact on the identity development of psychoanalytic candidates. Their primary finding was that supervisors who not only imparted knowledge, but also integrated "relationship competence" (p. 554) into their approach generated the biggest increases in identity development in their supervisees, as well as the greatest satisfaction for both supervisee and supervisor. The investigators concluded that psychoanalytic supervision should focus not only on the patient, but also on "the work of experiencing the supervision dyad" (p. 555), another confirmation of the focus on the supervisory relationship in the relational model.

All three of these studies offer evidence for the effectiveness of the relational model of psychodynamic supervision. Further evidence is available if we look outside the limited psychoanalytic research domain to the counseling psychology research.

THE COUNSELING PSYCHOLOGY SUPERVISION RESEARCH LITERATURE

Studying Expert Supervisors

Two teams of investigators from counseling psychology (Grant, Schofield, & Crawford, 2012; Nelson, Barnes, Evans, & Triggiano, 2008) interviewed, in depth, "expert" supervisors who identified with a broad range of theoretical orientations (psychodynamic, eclectic, developmental, family therapy, cognitive behavioral therapy, existential). The investigators sought to discover the skills and activities that most often characterized the supervisors' ways of working. Nelson et al. (2008) concluded that their "experts" were open to working with conflict, modeled interpersonal processing for their supervisees, were willing to acknowledge their shortcomings, and were ready to learn from their mistakes. Nelson et al. commented on these experts' "commitment to openness and desire to use the power relationship in supervision with care" (p. 177) and noted "a remarkable sense of humility" (p. 177) in the sample. Grant et al. (2012) observed that the expert supervisors they studied "demonstrated a high degree of reflectivity [on their impact on the supervisory relationship]" and that this reflectivity "was demonstrated within the context of a strongly relational approach" (p. 537). These supervisors were notably flexible in adjusting their approach to the needs of the supervisee and using their mistakes "to reflect deeply and develop more complex understandings" (p. 538). Grant et al. (2012) concluded: "Most models of supervision warn against addressing supervisees' personal issues. However, consistent with relational theory (Miehls, 2010), an important characteristic of our supervisors' expertise was their capacity to understand the relative contributions of personal and professional issues and to address them in a more integrated manner" (p. 538).

Findings from these two studies suggest that expert supervisors work in a way that is consistent with all three of the dimensions of the relational model of psychodynamic supervision. Both studies support (a) the relational view of the supervisor's authority, one of relative mutuality, with supervisors reflecting on their contributions to difficulties; (b) the relational view of the supervisor's mode of intervening, which includes working with tensions in the supervisory relationship; and (c) the relational view of what material should be discussed, which includes the parallel process, the supervisory relationship, and the personal as well as the professional.

The Importance of the Supervisory Relationship

Ladany and Bradley (2010), quoting Ellis and Ladany (1997), summed up the results of their comprehensive review of the supervision research literature in this way: "The supervisory relationship seems to be a key aspect of the supervision process, and it is likely to influence supervision process and outcome" (Ladany & Bradley, 2010, p. 361). Watkins (2013) summarized the supervision research on Bordin's[1] (1983) "supervisory working alliance," concluding that approximately 40 research studies, although primarily "ex post facto, cross-sectional, correlational, and nonprocess in nature" (p. 17), consistently showed that a good alliance predicts good things in supervision, and a bad alliance predicts bad things in supervision.

Indeed, a number of studies point to supervisee preference for supervisors who provide a "good" relationship. Riggs and Bretz (2006), using data from a survey of doctoral level interns, concluded that supervisees who perceived their supervisors as having a "secure" attachment style

---

[1]Bordin, now deceased, was my first supervisor. We worked together from 1971 to 1973. Bordin viewed the "working alliance" as a primary engine of change in the therapeutic and supervisory relationships and as a curative factor that transcended differences in theoretical approach. His emphasis on the relationship presaged relational psychoanalytic ideas, and I remain grateful to him for his contribution to my development as a psychotherapist and a supervisor.

had significantly more positive feelings about the supervisory task and the supervisory bond than did supervisees who did not perceive their supervisor as securely attached. Falender and Shafranske (2004) summarized research on what supervisees believe differentiates good from bad supervisors: trust and respect in the supervisory relationship, supervisor sensitivity to the supervisee's developmental needs, supervisor encouragement of supervisee autonomy, supervisor identification of discomfort and conflict in the supervisory relationship, supervisor willingness to clarify expectations and provide regular feedback, and supervisor nondefensive tolerance for negative supervisee feedback.

Supervisor Openness to Processing Conflict

Moskowitz and Rupert (1983) found that 38% of supervisees surveyed reported a major conflict with a supervisor. And yet, according to two studies that surveyed supervisees (Ladany, Hill, Corbett, & Nutt, 1996; Yourman & Farber, 1996), a significant number of supervisees reported that they felt too vulnerable to speak to their supervisors about their negative feelings about supervision. In these studies, as in a study by Gray, Ladany, Walker, and Ancis (2001), trainees preferred that the supervisor identify and initiate discussion of the conflict situation. Supervisees also reported that when they attempted to complain or raise an area of conflict with a supervisor, the supervisor too often responded defensively. Citing Gray and colleagues' (2001) study of counterproductive events in supervision, Falender and Shafranske (2004) also noted that supervisees feel unsafe in bringing up conflicts with their supervisors, and wish their supervisors would initiate such conversations.

These studies suggest that when a supervisor doesn't take into account the power differential in the relationship, the power differential creates a chilling effect in the supervisory relationship. When supervisors fail to invite negative feelings into the supervisory relationship,[2] supervisees

---

[2]Even psychoanalytically oriented supervisors who teach a relational or interpersonal model of treatment sometimes fail to appreciate the silencing effect of the power differential in supervision, or perhaps they fear transgressing the teach—treat boundary if they risk inquiring into the supervisee's experience of the supervisory relationship (Frawley-O'Dea & Sarnat, 2001; Hirsch, 1998).

withhold them to the detriment of their learning. (See chap. 1 on the consequences of Dewald's [1987] failure to explore his supervisee's negative feelings toward him.)

Task-Relevant Supervisor Disclosure

Research conducted by Ladany and Walker (2003) suggests that appropriate supervisor disclosure enhances the emotional-bond component of the supervisory alliance by communicating trust in the supervisee. Ladany and Lehrman-Waterman (1999) found that supervisor disclosures "relating to supervisors' emotional reactions to clients, their own counseling struggles and successes, personal feedback on the supervisory relationship, general professional experience, and didactic mentoring providing vicarious experiences" (p. 50) were facilitative, as long as supervisors didn't lose track of the supervisee's needs and become overly personal. This finding supports the concept of *mutuality in the context of asymmetry*: Task-related supervisor disclosure contributes to mutuality, whereas the supervisor's refraining from irrelevant personal disclosures upholds the necessary asymmetry of the supervisory dyad.

THE PSYCHODYNAMIC PSYCHOTHERAPY RESEARCH LITERATURE

If we look outside of the limited realm of supervision research, we find additional evidence for the pedagogical effectiveness of the relational model of psychodynamic supervision. We begin with psychodynamic psychotherapy. Supervisee emotional development is a primary learning objective in psychodynamic supervision. Emotional capacities that are important for psychodynamic supervisees to develop include providing empathic responsiveness and a secure and reliable relationship, maintaining a self-reflective stance under pressure, hearing a patient deeply and nonreactively while under attack, and refinding that capacity after losing it (Bion, 1962; Ogden, 2003, 2005; Safran & Muran, 2000; Sarnat, 2008, 2010, 2012). Although the tasks in psychotherapy and supervision are different in important ways, it stands to reason that factors that have been found to facilitate emotional development in patients may also facilitate emotional development in supervisees. What does the psychotherapy research literature tell us about how a psychotherapist facilitates the development of emotional capacities?

Psychotherapy outcome studies consistently point to a good therapeutic relationship as a predictor of positive outcome. Silverman (2005), in discussing the findings of an American Psychological Association task force on evidence-based practice, observed that the level of relationship skill of the psychotherapist is a more powerful predictor of outcome than technique. Orlinsky, Grawe, and Parks's (1994) meta-analysis of hundreds of psychotherapy process-outcome studies concluded that a good psychotherapeutic relationship—more than any specific form of intervention—was the strongest predictor of positive outcome and that effective psychotherapists were perceived by their clients as "empathic, affirmative, collaborative, and self-congruent" (p. 361). Their data also emphasized the effectiveness of psychotherapists who know how to create a secure attachment. This finding was reconfirmed by Crits-Christoph, Connelly Gibbons, and Mukherjee (2013) in their extensive, updated review of the psychotherapy process-outcome research. We can extrapolate from these conclusions that relationship capacities would also be essential for effective supervisors. These studies further support a model of supervision that emphasizes the relationship between supervisor and supervisee.

THE EDUCATION AND COGNITIVE PSYCHOLOGY
RESEARCH LITERATURE

Arguably, three learning tasks are essential for a developing psychoanalytic psychotherapist (Sarnat, 2012). These are acquiring usable, flexible, "procedural" knowledge; becoming expert at a variety of complex skills (such as developing a working alliance and identifying and working with transference and resistance); and developing a variety of emotional and relational capacities (such as those named in the previous section). Evidence from educational and cognitive psychology research suggests that several elements of a relational style of supervision facilitate the accomplishment of these learning tasks (Sarnat, 2012).

Beyond Manuals: Transmitting Procedural Knowledge

Some approaches to psychotherapy training depend upon carefully constructed training manuals. After working hard to create a good one, the Vanderbilt Psychotherapy Project team bumped up against the reality of manuals' limitations (Strupp & Binder, 1984). When they conducted research on the effectiveness of their manual (Strupp & Anderson, 1997), the team was struck by how radically individual psychotherapists varied in their capacity to implement its instructions. As Binder (1999) put it, "Interpersonal skills in establishing and maintaining an alliance with the patient are essential [in implementing this psychodynamic psychotherapy manual] ... however interpersonal skills are enormously difficult to teach" (p. 707). Binder concluded that the challenge was to find a way to help trainees connect the abstract, declarative knowledge they gained from manuals to their lived experience—that is, to transform it into procedural knowledge.

Cabaniss (2012), in her review of cognitive science and education research, concurred with Binder (1999). She concluded that the most effective educational experiences for adult learners—experiences that transmit actively useful knowledge that is accessible in the consulting room—are those that are directly salient to the learner and are problem-centered, interactive, and affectively rich. These are precisely the kinds of educational experiences that characterize psychoanalytic supervision. It is for this reason, perhaps, that supervision has been called psychoanalytic education's "signature pedagogy" (Watkins, 2014). These qualities are even more characteristic of a relational, as opposed to classically didactic, approach to psychoanalytic supervision. All psychodynamic supervisors invite supervisees to bring clinical material that is salient to them and centered on the immediate problems that concern them. However, a supervisor working from a relational model is likely to also create an affectively rich and highly interactive supervisory environment.

Building Complex Skills and Emotional/Relational Capacities

Cabaniss's (2012) research review suggested that an experiential supervisory environment is best suited to helping a psychotherapist develop complex skills and emotional/relational capacities. Didactic methods and skill-practice methods do not suffice. Most trainees can be taught to *identify* the major transference dynamic in a transcript or process note through such methods. (See chap. 3 for more on teaching such skills.) But direct experience is necessary to prepare a supervisee to *work with* transference in an actual psychotherapy hour. Knowing when to bring up the transference and when to stay within the patient's derivative communication; knowing when to speak from *within* the transference and when to speak *about* the transference—or whether to say nothing at all at a given moment—requires complex capacities that are impossible to teach through instruction or structured exercises (Sarnat, 2012). A supervisee's experience with his own psychotherapist facilitates such learning, although there are limits: One's patients' transferences are not the same as one's own, and one's analyst is not a perfect model for oneself. Experiences with one's psychotherapist cannot substitute for the specific-to-the-patient-and-to-the-supervisee learning that transpires within the supervisory relationship.

Opportunity for such learning presents itself when a supervisee identifies with his patient's transference and unconsciously carries it into the supervisory relationship—the supervisee "channeling" his patient and bringing "a parallel process" into supervision. In so doing, the supervisee confronts the supervisor with the same interpersonal challenge by which he has felt stymied in his relationship with the patient. If the supervisor can effectively address these dynamics in the supervisory relationship, the supervisee directly experiences an intervention just at the moment that he is maximally primed to learn from it.

THE NEUROSCIENCE RESEARCH LITERATURE

Neuroscience and Teaching Psychodynamic Psychotherapists

Divino and Moore (2010) drew upon neuroscience research to design what they considered to be an optimal classroom environment for teaching psychoanalytic psychotherapists. They noted that neuroscience research shows that experiences that stimulate multiple regions of the brain result in the most effective learning. Therefore, they designed the class to activate the left hemisphere of the brain (the part of the brain that processes cognition and language), as well as the right hemisphere, midbrain, and limbic areas (the parts of the brain that process nonverbal impressions and affects). To do so, they made the classroom experiential in a variety of ways. They designed their lectures to be personally relevant to their students and brought the material into the here and now. For example, in teaching about the brain and anxiety, they focused on performance pressures and competitive anxieties that students generally struggle with. The co-instructors also openly processed conflicts that arose between them to provide an in vivo model for the most effective way of working with interpersonally "hot" material. However, they were careful not to make the affective environment "too hot" because research indicates that too much affect disrupts learning.

The pedagogical parallel between Divino and Moore's (2010) classroom situation and the supervisory environment created by a relational supervisor is apparent: A personally relevant focus, experiential engagement with the supervisee, and open processing of conflicts in the supervisory relationship are all aspects of the relational approach. Divino and Moore asserted that their classroom was "evidence-based." Their evidence, then, supports the relational model of supervision as well.

Neuroscience, Psychodynamic Psychotherapy, and Supervision

Schore (2011) reviewed neuroscience research for findings relevant to effective psychotherapy practice. Like Divino and Moore (2010), Schore concluded that to stimulate emotional growth, it is essential not to neglect patients' right brains. More specifically, he advocated for "right brain to right brain" communication between patient and psychotherapist— a connection that, he emphasized, goes beyond words. He concluded from neuroscience research that it is not so much what a psychotherapist *says* but how a psychotherapist is implicitly and subjectively *with* the patient, especially during affectively stressful moments, that makes the difference between successful and unsuccessful treatment.

These understandings from neuroscience have had an impact on the practice of psychodynamic psychotherapy, enlarging its technical repertoire as well as the scope of patients for whom it is effective. This expansion in treatment model demands, in turn, an expansion of supervisory model: A supervisee learns best to work with nonsemantic elements in psychotherapy when he experiences such work in supervision. Frawley-O'Dea (1997a, 1997b; Frawley-O'Dea & Sarnat, 2001), in fact, began to develop her ideas about relational supervision specifically to address her dissatisfaction with the too-limited (patient-centered, verbally focused) approach of one of her supervisors during her psychoanalytic training. She needed help in working with the inchoate states of mind, enactments, and intense affects that her patients brought to the analytic encounter, and that paralleled into the supervisory relationship.

Ulmer (2011) reviewed the neuroscience literature for indications of what might make for an effective supervisory relationship, and her conclusions echoed and expanded upon Schore's (2011). She found evidence that contemplative states of mind (the calm states that come from meditative practices) provide a powerful vehicle for helping the other to process difficult nonsemantic therapeutic material. This suggests that the atmosphere created by the supervisor—one of spaciousness (Ogden, 2005), receptivity, and calmness—has an impact on the supervisee's ability to emotionally settle and then to think and feel deeply and creatively about the patient.

Divino and Moore's, Schore's, and Ulmer's readings of the neuroscience research offer additional confirmation of the values and methods of a relational model of psychodynamic supervision. Creating lively, here-and-now learning opportunities; attending to nonsemantic, right-brain material, together with left-brain semantic and cognitive material; and caring as much about the emotional environment one creates in supervision as about the conceptual content that one is teaching, are all supported by this literature.

CONCLUSION

Findings from the psychoanalytic and counseling supervision literatures consistently confirm the importance of the supervisory relationship, including working in the here and now in that relationship and making links between what goes on in the supervisory relationship and what is going on in the clinical relationship. These literatures also provide support for emphasizing supervisor "relationship competence," specifically singling out such qualities as openness to working with conflict, the capacity to reflect on one's impact on the supervisory relationship, comfort working with personal and professional issues together, and providing a secure attachment. When surveyed, supervisees consistently prefer supervisors who offer what they feel are "good" relationships: relationships of mutual trust, supervisor sensitivity, willingness to identify and discuss areas of tension, and nondefensiveness. The supervisor's capacity to create a good supervisory alliance repeatedly has been shown to predict good things in supervision.

In the psychotherapy research literature, the psychotherapist's level of relationship skill predicts outcome more powerfully than does any technical approach. A good therapeutic relationship is, in fact, the strongest predictor of outcome, again supporting a relationship-focus in supervision.

Findings from research in the related disciplines of cognitive psychology and education provide evidence that didactic teaching in supervision is not enough. Experiential, relationship-based teaching is most effective in developing procedural knowledge and emotional/relational capacities, which are both essential for a psychodynamic psychotherapist. The neuroscience research further confirms the importance of an approach that includes the right brain: An affectively rich, calm, and experientially focused supervisory environment is optimal for teaching and learning.

A coherent picture emerges from these literatures of an effective supervisor who works in a way that is consistent to a surprising degree with the relational model of psychodynamic supervision. She has a view of her own authority that leads her to ask her supervisee about negative experiences in supervision, and she contributes to her supervisee's feeling of safety in discussing them because she takes responsibility for her contribution to difficulties (Dimension 1). That supervisor expands the material that is discussed beyond the supervisee's verbal report of the hour to include affects and enactments and other nonsemantic elements, and is attentive to how these appear in the here and now of the supervisory relationship. She understands the importance of experiential learning (Dimension 2). Finally, the supervisor is aware that her mode of participation with her supervisee—not just the wisdom she communicates to the supervisee but how she is *with* her supervisee—is essential to the supervisee's growth and development (Dimension 3).

In the next chapter, I discuss how the methods of the relational psychodynamic supervisor derive from the essential dimensions of the relational model and are backed by the evidence presented in this chapter. What methods contribute to the mutuality of the supervisory relationship despite its intrinsic asymmetries of power and authority? What methods allow the supervisory dyad to enlarge the breadth and depth of material with which they work? What methods allow the supervisor to make appropriate use of her clinical skills on behalf of teaching?

3

Supervisory Methods and Techniques

Having considered the essential dimensions of the relational model of psychodynamic supervision in chapter 1 and having looked at the evidence that supports the effectiveness of this approach in chapter 2, I now elaborate some of the methods and techniques that are distinctive to a relational psychodynamic approach.[1] The specific details of what relational supervisors do vary a great deal from supervisor to supervisor. For this reason, after sketching out some general themes, I do not attempt to speak for all relational supervisors but instead offer some of the specifics of how I work. I consider how the essential dimensions of the model—the relational supervisor's view of authority, of what material to include in the supervisory discussion, and of her mode of participation—translate into what the supervisor actually does. I start by articulating what is different about relational methods and techniques in general. Then I discuss several

---

[1] For a broader perspective on methods in supervision—that is, a perspective that is not specifically relational—see *Guidelines for Clinical Supervision in Health Service Psychology* (APA, 2014).

http://dx.doi.org/10.1037/14802-004
Supervision Essentials for Psychodynamic Psychotherapies, by J. E. Sarnat
Copyright © 2016 by the American Psychological Association.

specific methods: initial assessment, negotiating how to work together, working with a range of supervisee requests, matching the form in which material is presented to the request, evaluation, and documentation. Finally, I consider what is distinctive about relational case conference.

WHAT IS DISTINCTIVE ABOUT RELATIONAL METHODS AND TECHNIQUES?

A relational supervisor's ways of working express the essential dimensions of the model. She prioritizes methods and techniques that encourage supervisee expressiveness and authenticity, methods that encourage the supervisee to be as open as possible in presenting material and disclosing his actual difficulties and concerns. This means paying attention to supervisee anxiety and shame and acknowledging one's own conflicts and anxieties and the hurtful things one may do as a result. Rather than expecting the supervisee to comply with her ideas about the patient and technique, as a more classical supervisor might, the relational supervisor draws out the supervisee's ideas and is interested in exploring differences.

Like most supervisors, the relational psychodynamic supervisor values methods that develop a sense of partnership in which both members commit to pursuing the same goals—what is commonly called the *supervisory alliance* (Fleming & Benedek, 1966; Watkins, 2013). But the relational supervisor's interest in the supervisory relationship goes beyond encouraging collaboration and repairing ruptures. She is also alert to the possibility that what is going on in the supervisory relationship may reflect dynamics that have paralleled in from the clinical relationship or that she herself may have introduced. In addition, she views working with her supervisee's feelings toward her as an opportunity to model clinical technique and facilitate emotional and relational growth in the supervisee. She understands that experiential learning, which is facilitated by working in the supervisory relationship, is the most useful kind, and she appreciates her supervisee's needs for regulation of affect, security, and the provision of theory to help contain anxiety.

The relational supervisor's approach to technique is extremely flexible. For example, although she teaches about the patient and technique, she is prepared to let go of didactic methods when they prove ineffective or insufficient and to turn her attention to what is emerging in the supervisory relationship. In addition, she wants to enhance her supervisee's way of working rather than trying to make the supervisee work exactly as she does.

The relational supervisor crafts her method to suit the specific needs of the supervisory dyad, finding ways of working that suit them uniquely. Understanding and adapting to the supervisee's psychology is as important to the relational supervisor as understanding and adapting to the patient's psychology. Supervisor and supervisee explore the supervisee's learning needs, entering into explicit and implicit negotiations about how to work together.

SOME SPECIFIC METHODS TYPICAL OF RELATIONAL SUPERVISION

Assessment in the First Meeting

The supervisor meets the supervisee with questions in mind, such as: Where is this supervisee developmentally?[2] What anxieties and countertransference issues are most prominent? How available is this supervisee to explore himself? How much clinical training has the supervisee received, and what have his previous experiences in supervision been like? The answers to these questions contribute to the supervisor's selection of methods. In addition, the supervisor considers what methods fit best with the policies and expectations of the particular clinical setting and/or educational organization in which the supervision takes place, be it agency or training clinic. Finally, the supervisor considers her own needs, competencies, and preferences, asking herself questions such as: What supervisory methods are process-consistent with the clinical approach that I am trying to teach? What methods are most comfortable for me, given my personality, training, and experience? What kinds of responses

---

[2]For an empirically based and more general exploration of supervisee development, see Rønnestad and Skovholt (2013).

does this particular supervisee evoke from me, and what does he not evoke? How is that influencing—and how should it influence—my way of working in this dyad?

Negotiating a Way to Work Together

What follows is a description of some things I generally consider doing in initial supervisory sessions. I do not have a strict protocol for how I begin.

If a supervisee has requested me, I may ask about his expectations about working with me and spend time discussing those. If the supervisee and I are newly acquainted, I may try to explore the goodness of fit between our preferences for how to work in supervision. I want my supervisee to feel heard by me and that he has taken an active part in defining what we are doing together. I want a partner in supervision.

Although I invite my supervisee to join me in discussing how we may best work together, at the same time, I let him know in some way that I take ultimate responsibility for assessing and addressing his learning needs, as well as for evaluation. I thus try to communicate my view of the supervisory relationship as one of mutuality in the context of asymmetry.

The *Guidelines for Clinical Supervision in Health Service Psychology* (American Psychological Association [APA], 2014) state that it is "preferable" to provide a written supervisory contract (Domain G, Standard 4, p. 25). However, I, like many psychoanalysts, prefer to reach a verbal understanding with my supervisee unless a training organization specifically asks to me provide a written one. A verbal contract is more readily individualized and more readily amended, as conditions require, and it is more personal and less bureaucratic, contributing to the environment of intimacy that I value in supervision. I do, however, maintain notes about what we verbally agree to and periodically refer back to them with my supervisee. This becomes important in those rare situations when supervisees experience serious difficulties or when supervisor and supervisee have a serious disagreement (see chap. 5).

Working With the Supervisee's Request

Establishing specific, transparent learning objectives has been shown to be a significant contributor to effective psychoanalytic education (Cabaniss, 2008; Moga & Cabaniss, 2014). I try to approach the issue of learning objectives by working with the supervisee's *request*, a term that emphasizes the supervisee's felt need. If a supervisee feels a need for help with something, I see it as my job to facilitate transforming the request into an appropriate goal for our work together. I help my supervisee to elaborate and clarify his request for supervision, listening for the broader learning needs that underlie the felt need and opening a process of negotiation about what we will try to work on in supervision. A few examples illustrate the range of supervisee requests and how I might respond to them. Beginners generally make different kinds of requests than do more experienced supervisees.

Beginner Requests

Beginning supervisees—those who are in what Rønnestad and Skovholt (2003) call "The Beginning Student Phase"—often indicate concerns about the basics of initiating a psychodynamic psychotherapy, such as:

- "I have only worked in crisis settings and have no idea what to do with a client who is not experiencing an active crisis."
- "I am experienced with cognitive behavioral therapy, but I feel lost if I'm not giving homework and helping to change internal scripts."
- "I am having trouble getting started with clients. The patients I have met with in initial interviews haven't wanted to stay in treatment with me."

It is extremely stressful for a novice psychodynamic psychotherapist to be thrown in with a patient when he has very little idea what to do. I therefore tend to respond quite directly to such requests, teaching the basics of how to structure the therapeutic situation, how to listen, how to encourage the patient to keep talking, and how to present material in supervision. Some readers might be surprised that a relational psychodynamic

supervisor would offer concrete advice, but a relational supervisor adapts
to the specifics of the emotional and interpersonal situation, and providing direct guidance can be essential to decreasing a beginning supervisee's
anxiety. I will intentionally refrain from the kind of open-ended exploration that I engage in with more advanced clinicians because it can make
beginners more anxious rather than less (Josephs, 1990). I also try to nor-
malize my supervisee's feelings of helplessness and inadequacy.

Intermediate-Level Requests

Supervisees who are somewhat more experienced—those who lie some-
where between The Beginning Student Phase and The Advanced Student
Phase in Rønnestad and Skovholt's (2003) model—make requests that
indicate that, although they may have gotten started in their psychodynamic work with patients, certain basic issues still concern them:

- "I have trouble formulating my patients' difficulties, and I need help
  applying theory to my work."
- "I don't know how to use my formulation to guide my listening and
  intervening."
- "I seem to start out fine with clients, but then my therapies get stuck.
  The process stays 'chatty,' and I don't know what to do to help things
  deepen."
- "I keep getting caught up in the manifest content and am not sure what
  'listening for the unconscious' means."
- "Can you help me to identify the transference and figure out what to
  do with it?"

From these kinds of requests, I infer that my supervisee, although
in need of significant supervisory help, is not a beginner and therefore probably is somewhat less anxious and likely will neither need nor
benefit from the same degree of concrete input. However, supervisees
making such requests may need to practice specific psychoanalytic skills
in supervision.

So, for example, to help a supervisee develop the capacity to identify
unconscious transference material, I might ask him to extract the main

theme from the manifest content of the presented hour. Then I would ask my supervisee to think about how that theme might be related to what he imagines might be on the patient's mind about her relationship to her therapist. Then we will use this material to find words for interpreting the transference, if doing so seems like it would facilitate the process. In this exercise, I lead my supervisee, step by step, through a process that I go through semiautomatically in my own clinical work. Practice of this kind is far more pedagogically effective than simply telling a supervisee what the supervisor thinks is the primary transference theme in the session and expecting the supervisee to figure it out on his own the next time. Unfortunately, the latter approach is an all-too-common psychodynamic supervisory strategy (see Cabaniss, 2012).

Implicit Requests

Sometimes learning issues emerge only indirectly in supervision, rather than in an explicit request. Examples include the following:

- "I have had some trouble collecting fees, and the director of the clinic says it is becoming a problem."
- "I have a patient who keeps canceling. I didn't talk about it with my previous supervisor because I actually don't think it is an issue."

These requests come from my own experience. With the first request, I began by helping my supervisee to acknowledge that he, not only the clinic director, thought the fee situation was a problem. Once the supervisee was able to take ownership of the issue, we could begin to understand how his conflicts and anxiety were expressed in his difficulty collecting fees. With the supervisee in the second example, I had some initial work to do before we could agree that there was a problem. Then we had to work out whether the supervisee wanted and needed my help with it (although, naturally, *I* thought she did). (See chap. 6 for further discussion of this supervisory vignette with my supervisee, Andrea.) With both of these supervisees, the request required that we first negotiate a supervisory focus and establish an alliance vis-à-vis that focus before we could arrive at a mutually meaningful learning objective.

Requests Made by Advanced Students

Supervisees who are in The Advanced Student Phase (Rønnestad & Skovholt, 2003) of learning psychodynamic psychotherapy are engaged in the process of developing complex skills and learning how to employ them skillfully, as well developing sophisticated emotional and relational capacities (Sarnat, 2012). These competencies cannot be systematically broken down and practiced in the way one can help a supervisee to formulate a transference theme. As research cited in chapter 2 suggests, supervisors can facilitate the development of such capacities by working with the here and now of the supervisory relationship, although the "bread and butter" supervisory activities of trying to understand the patient and teaching technique continue as well.

Once a psychodynamic treatment is underway, therapeutically useful enactments involving patient, supervisee, and supervisor are generated intermittently, and these are taken up and processed in supervision. A back-and-forth flow from didactic teaching, to processing of enactment, and back to teaching, often characterizes my work with supervisees who have moved beyond the beginner stage. The supervisory hour that is excerpted in chapter 4 gives an example of this kind of work. In this hour, my supervisee, Jane, an advanced student, enacted in supervision a troublesome dynamic from the presented treatment, unconsciously providing me with a taste of the frustration she felt when her patient rejected her efforts at interpretation. When I realized this, I let go of trying to teach about what I thought was going on between Jane and her patient and, instead, attended to the dynamic in our relationship. I offered her a direct experience of how a "helper," be it psychotherapist or supervisor, may shift gears with a person who is not finding the "helper" to be helpful. Jane learned through this experience something that I could not teach her through direct instruction and that she could not have learned in her own psychotherapy, no matter how helpful her psychotherapist might be. The direct parallel between Jane's situation with me and her patient's situation with her allowed Jane to experience something in supervision that was highly salient to her, and my on-the-spot intervention facilitated her growth as a psychotherapist. As the enactment resolved, I returned later in the hour to a "teaching" mode.

Advanced students also request help with the emotions that are evoked in working with particular patients. Here, too, Jane may serve as an example. She let me know that in her work with several of her patients—whom she had been seeing for several years at two or more sessions per week—she had become intensely emotionally involved and didn't know how to use her feelings to facilitate her patients' progress. I asked her to be as candid as possible in supervision about her feelings in these therapeutic relationships. Jane did so. The transcript in chapter 4 shows how we worked to help her to learn from her emotions and use them to help her patient.

Deciding in What Form Clinical Material Will Be Presented[3]

I want the form in which my supervisees present material to fit their request and their learning needs. For this reason, methods of presentation vary. Here are some of the most important ones.

Supervisee-Generated Questions

Often beginners, in particular, feel a need for immediate answers to questions that trouble them from their most recent clinical hour. I accommodate to such needs. Doing so gives the supervisee some control in supervision, despite often feeling frighteningly out of control in his clinical sessions. I do not insist upon process notes with anxious beginners; initially writing them may feel onerous and overly exposing. In any case, beginners are often not available to use process notes to reflect on the flow of a session because they are operating in crisis mode. Only after my supervisee gets his "sea legs" can we begin to look at what is happening in the sessions in a broader and more reflective way.

---

[3]For an instructive general discussion of the advantages of various ways of presenting material in supervision, see Bernard and Goodyear (2014).

Audiovisual Recording

I find audio recordings[4] useful in supervision but do not always request them. If a supervisee does not express an interest in recording, and I have the sense that our work is meaningful and rich without including such recordings in our sessions, I will not necessarily use them, although I always invite my supervisees to bring in recordings. However, if a supervisee expresses concern about how he is speaking to the patient, feels a desire for me to experience the patient and the interaction firsthand, or wants me to help him to understand what was going on in an hour that he found particularly confusing and could not record properly in his notes, I suggest listening to the recording.

Whenever a supervisee plays recorded material, I am mindful of the narcissistic exposure and risk involved. To protect our alliance, I encourage the supervisee to decide what part of the tape is played and what issues we discuss, especially when we first begin. I invite my supervisee's associations to the material and add my own later, with discretion. Supervisees sometimes feel relief when their "secret transgression" or "private failure" is shared with me and I respond in a nonshaming way. Over time, as trust develops between us, most supervisees become comfortable relinquishing some control over what we discuss, and then I begin to bring up issues that seem important to me but of which the supervisee appeared unaware.

One supervisee chose to play a series of excerpts from recordings over a period of weeks, raising questions about them that became progressively focused and risk taking. For example, he went from "Is something going on here that I am missing?" to "I know I am caught up in reacting to manifest content again in this session. What do you think is going on unconsciously in this passage, and why can't I hear it?" A second question evolved from "I am worried that I am talking too much in this passage. Do you think that is true?" to "I know that I am talking too much, and I wonder why it happened at this point in the session. Can you

---

[4]Because I supervise in my private office and do not currently have equipment for playing videos—and few of my supervisees have equipment for making video recordings—I request audio recording. With improvements in technology, that may soon be changing.

help me to understand what triggered me?" This progression reflected this supervisee's growing insight into himself and the development of an analytic attitude (that is, an attitude of nonjudgmental curiosity) toward himself. My accepting attitude toward his recordings (always easier when the supervisee is already monitoring himself!) contributed to that progression. As a supervisor, it is my hope that my supervisees will internalize my analytic attitude and carry it into the clinical hour, leading to an increase in their capacity to bear and work with their countertransference responses.

Occasionally I will insist on recordings if I feel they are necessary for me to do my job responsibly. If I have concerns about a supervisee's work, I will be direct about that, and I also make myself available to discuss my supervisee's anxieties about what the tapes may reveal. If, when I hear recorded material, my concerns are confirmed, I will inform the training institution about the student's difficulties and do what is necessary to make sure the patient receives ethical care. But my first responsibility is to speak to my supervisee, in a nonshaming way, about his difficulties. (See the section on evaluation in this chapter and also chap. 5 for more on working with supervisees with serious difficulties.)

Process Notes

Process notes are the preferred modality among psychodynamic supervisors for working with intermediate-level and advanced supervisees. When we are trying to deepen the supervisee's appreciation of unconscious communication or attempting to get hold of something that is being enacted in the clinical hours, it is often productive to get a feel for the flow of the full session or a series of sessions via such notes because they condense the process into a manageable unit. When I supervise psychoanalytic candidates, we focus intensively on a single patient whom the candidate sees three or four times weekly, and I routinely (although not exclusively) work with process notes.

I teach the art of taking process notes to many supervisees because the quality of their notes will determine the quality of supervisory and consultative help they will be able to receive throughout their careers. I acknowledge the inevitability of the supervisee's preconceptions shaping what he remembers and writes down, as well as the common phenomenon of discovering that the most loaded interactions for the supervisee, when the supervisee was in a state of arousal, may be missing altogether from memory. (If this happens repeatedly, taping may be helpful.) I suggest that supervisees track the major transitions in material as best they can, then fill in the details from there. I also encourage them to summarize, rather than report in detail, passages that are repetitive to capture the psychological heart of the material without wasting precious note-taking or supervisory time. Making such choices teaches the supervisee to be mindful about the meaning and function of the patient's associations. Yet I also try to help my supervisee accept that there will be periods when he stops thinking and remembering and just goes into the flow of the hour, and his notes will reflect this. Supervisees' own fantasies, bodily sensations, and reveries (Ogden, 1994) are also valuable to include as a source of right-brain to right-brain communication about the transference-countertransference. Finally, I encourage supervisees to pay attention to and try to note how the patient responds after the supervisee offers interpretations, so that we may think together about how the patient is unconsciously experiencing the intervention and whether or not it seems effective.

Supervisee Personal Disclosure

A rigid expectation that process notes be presented in each supervisory hour can preclude other important conversations. I make it clear that I am open to a variety of ways of using our time together and also to a variety of topics of conversation. Although I am mindful of the privacy rights of supervisees,[5] I find that many *initiate* personal conversations with me. If a supervisee raises a personal topic, I start with the assumption that there is a reason that he is bringing the issue up with me, rather than

---

[5] Standard 7.04 of the APA *Ethical Principles of Psychologists and Code of Conduct* (2010) states that supervisors do not require supervisees to disclose personal information unless the training program has identified this requirement at the time of admission or "the information is necessary to evaluate or obtain assistance for students whose personal problems could reasonably be judged to be preventing them from performing their training- or professionally related activities in a competent manner or posing a threat to the (sic) students or others" (p. 9).

bringing it to his friend or psychotherapist. I look for how the issue may be related to my supervisee's work with patients, his ability to collaborate in our supervisory relationship, and/or his professional development. I am receptive when supervisees want me to know about difficulties they are experiencing in their personal lives. Developing the capacity to work competently during periods of personal upheaval is a challenge for every psychotherapist. I view the willingness to request help during such periods as an important capacity. All psychotherapists are human, despite the pressure that some patients put on us to be otherwise.

However, if the issue requires more time and attention than is realistic for me to provide in supervision, I will raise the issue of personal psychotherapy. If my supervisee is in treatment, I may inquire whether he feels he is getting the help he needs from his psychotherapist. If he is not in treatment, I will suggest that he consider it. Concurrent psychotherapy (or analysis) makes an enormous difference in the development of a psychodynamic psychotherapist. (See chap. 7 in *The Supervisory Relationship* [Frawley-O'Dea & Sarnat, 2001] for a detailed discussion of how supervision is different when a supervisee is—or is not—in concurrent personal psychotherapy.)

Of course, it also sometimes happens that a supervisee will use personal disclosure as a way of avoiding talking about his work with patients; just as in treatment, in supervision almost anything can be used in the service of resistance. If I sense that resistance is in play, I may comment on it or may simply recommend that we return to discussing the work with the patient.

Evaluating the Supervisee

I generally introduce the issue of evaluation during the first supervisory hour. In my experience, if evaluation is not taken up directly by the supervisor, supervisees worry about it silently and often do not perceive the supervisory relationship to be safe enough to allow for candid self-expression. I acknowledge that it is hard for supervisees to be open about their personal feelings, challenges, and difficulties with someone who will also be evaluating them. I let them know, however, that I respect supervisees who are open to discussing their inevitable difficulties, that I am very much aware of my own, and that they can depend on me to provide them with direct feedback before I speak to anyone else.

Frawley-O'Dea and I (Frawley-O'Dea & Sarnat, 2001) included in our book an example of how we might address evaluation during the initial session of supervision. We emphasized our respect for supervisees who are open about their lack of knowledge and difficulties rather than trying to present themselves as highly competent. We invited their feedback about our supervisory helpfulness and acknowledged the impact of the power differential between us. Finally, we noted that conversations about evaluation can be affected by dynamics in the supervised case.

This way of talking about evaluation[6] derives from the relational view of the supervisor's authority: emphasizing mutual vulnerability, acknowledging the asymmetries of power and authority in the supervisory relationship, and affirming the primacy of the supervisor's bond to the supervisee while also acknowledging her alliance with the sponsoring training organization and her obligation to the supervised patient. This is a complex balance of messages that may not be fully absorbed in the moment but one that is important to have articulated *before* engaging in evaluative conversations. (For discussion of the ethical issues raised by evaluation, see chap. 7.)

Documentation

Supervisors have an ethical obligation to keep notes just as psychotherapists do (APA, 2010; Thomas, 2010). Supervisors need to think about their notes in terms of the different purposes they may serve. Notes for the supervisor's personal use are quite different from notes that are intended for potential consumption by others.

Notes for Personal Use

I take notes to support my not-always-reliable memory. I document anything that happens that I might want to return to in another session, as

---

[6] For more general discussions of evaluation in supervision, see Welfare (2010) and Bernard and Goodyear (2014).

well as some basic information about each presented patient. When a supervisee presents process notes to me, I may record the flow of the hour as an aid to analyzing the session with my supervisee.

I also write down the learning goals that my supervisee and I formulate together; I refer back to these periodically to keep myself and my supervisee on track. When previously stated goals no longer seem relevant, supervisee development may have occurred, and it may be time to define new goals. Alternatively, my supervisee and I may have developed a clearer understanding of what the appropriate goals actually are for this supervisee and need to revise them accordingly. If, when I refer to an earlier noted goal, I realize that we have lost track of it, this may signal that we have been pulled into an enactment, and returning to the noted goal can "wake us up" from such unconscious involvement.

I take more detailed notes of the to-and-fro of the supervisory conversation when I am planning to present to colleagues for consultation on my supervisory work to get perspective on the supervisory process in which I am embedded. These notes can be helpful in the same way that clinical process notes are helpful in communicating to a supervisor the detail of what is actually going on between the participants. At times I can also serve as my own consultant by reviewing such notes.

Notes for Consumption by Others

When issues of safety or legal/ethical issues come up in a case, I take formal notes that I assume may eventually be read by others. I want to document that my supervisee and I have taken the issue seriously and have each attended to it appropriately. I also document progress my supervisee makes and difficulties that my supervisee is having so that I may draw upon this material when writing evaluations. Providing specific data is essential to evaluation documents and evaluation conversations.

It is also part of the supervisor's legal/ethical responsibility to ensure that the supervisee is taking appropriate chart notes. I help my supervisee to differentiate those notes from process notes or other notes that he may take for his personal use, such as to prepare for supervision.

CASE CONFERENCE: SUPERVISING IN A GROUP

We now turn to supervising in a group, the activity that is called "case conference."[7] As with individual supervision, there are relational and non-relational psychodynamic models of case conference.

Nonrelational Case Conference

Supervising in a group is popular in agency settings in part because it allows a single supervisor to oversee the work of multiple students or staff members at once. Some supervision groups are convened to ensure that staff provide competent services when there is neither the time nor the money for individual supervision. These kinds of groups serve a primarily administrative function and therefore can fail to take advantage of the group situation's full potential for teaching and learning.

But even some psychodynamically oriented case conferences that are convened for educational purposes fail to take advantage of the full potential of the group situation. These case conferences are conducted in a manner similar to teaching in conventional classrooms: After a case is presented, the supervisor, like a classroom teacher, may call for some group comment and then give her conceptualization of the case, using the case material to teach her own version of theory and technique. In this kind of case conference, what I call a classical model case conference, the leader's ideas take priority, and group process is not addressed. (See the example of "Ken" in Frawley-O'Dea and Sarnat [2001], chap. 9.)

Relational Psychodynamic Case Conference

A relational psychodynamic case conference is a more complex, experiential, and engaged undertaking. The leader may offer her perspective on the patient and technique, but the conference is structured to facilitate working with unconscious material in the here and now of the group setting, involving participants in doing so. Participants are encouraged to notice their feelings and fantasies as the group discusses the case. Elements

---

[7] Some of the content of this section is adapted from chapter 9 in *The Supervisory Relationship* (Frawley-O'Dea & Sarnat, 2001).

of the unconscious process between the presenter and his patient, elements that the presenter could not communicate in his verbal narrative, often parallel into the conference's affective experience and are replayed in the group interaction. It is the supervisor's job, in addition to using the material to demonstrate points of theory and technique and raising questions for discussion, to help group members make meaning of their experience and learn from it.

Bion's Theory of Groups and the Relational Case Conference Leader

As must already be clear, the leader of a relationally oriented case conference will be group savvy. For me, a psychoanalyst, familiarity with Bion's (1961) theory of groups is an important part of the skill set (Burka, Sarnat, & St. John, 2007). Understanding Bion's concept of *group-as-a-whole* makes it possible for the leader to listen to members' comments as an expression of the group unconscious in addition to hearing members' comments as expressions of each individual. When the group supervisor offers her understanding of how individuals may be expressing group-as-a-whole dynamics, she enhances participants' awareness of what their individual *valence* is—that is, what role they are particularly inclined to play in the group and what kinds of feelings and fantasies they are likely to express on behalf of the group.

Bion's ideas about two distinct modes of group function are also helpful to the relational case conference leader: Groups can at any given moment function either mostly realistically, in what Bion calls *work group* mode, or largely based on fantasy, in what Bion calls *basic assumption group* mode (Burka et al., 2007). When operating in work group mode, members of the group attend to their own experience and use their experience to learn the art of psychotherapy, taking a realistic approach to the task. When a case conference is caught up in basic assumption life, it becomes organized around fantasy assumptions, loses touch with the demands of reality, and becomes distracted from the group's defined task.

From Bion's perspective, the goal of the group leader is twofold. First, she works to maintain—or to reestablish when it is lost—work-group mentality. She does this, in part, by attending to the anxieties that are inevitably evoked in the group, trying through her participation to contain them sufficiently so that group members may process their experiences and associations on behalf of learning. Second, the supervisor helps the group to observe its own experience as a way of gaining insight into the dynamics of the patient and the therapeutic relationship. Basic assumption dynamics in case conference are seen as a form of group resistance, but they may also be viewed as enactments stemming from the presented case, an important source of information for analytic processing.

In case conference, as in all educational situations, the supervisor strives to encourage thinking, understanding, and making meaning rather than merely enacting unconscious primitive states. But accepting the inevitability of primitive states of mind arising in case conference can allow a depth of learning that is not otherwise possible. A relational case conference leader works to create a learning environment in which affects and other nonsemantic experiences evoked by the patient, presenter, or leader can be experienced and expressed by members without criticism or accusation of being "unprofessional."

Working with unconscious group dynamics is not the only case conference leader activity. The relational case conference leader may also teach about the patient and technique, as long as the group is available to think. I offer my own interpretations about the case material but do not comment from a position of objective authority. I communicate that although I may have more experience and more theoretical knowledge, I am participating through my own subjectivity, and I cannot claim to know what is "true" about the patient any more than any other participant. I also explicitly acknowledge that my ideas about technique are based on my own particular way of working, which will not—and should not—be the same as the way of working of any other psychotherapist.

In *The Supervisory Relationship* (Frawley-O'Dea & Sarnat, 2001), Frawley-O'Dea and I provided an example of how a relationally oriented case conference leader works. I summarize the vignette here.

Vignette

A psychoanalytic candidate, Mary, was presenting Lisa to an initial meeting of a case conference. When Mary matter-of-factly elaborated disturbing details of Lisa's practice of self-mutilation, group members fell into silent shock. When the supervisor drew out members' reactions, they expressed repulsion, terror, fatigue, and difficulty thinking. Some members of the group then became critical of how emotionally out of touch with her patient and the group Mary seemed. Other members of the group remained silent. The supervisor made space for members' feelings, but also insisted that the group focus on understanding why things were unfolding as they were in the case conference, rather than giving advice to Mary or criticizing her about how she was handling the treatment. Both the critical and the silent members then shifted into trying to make sense of their reactions to Mary's presentation.

In the following meeting, Mary was able to reflect on how out of touch she had been with Lisa and with the material she had presented the previous week. It was almost as though she had awakened from a kind of trance. In the clinical session she presented in this second case conference meeting, she seemed much more connected to Lisa. Members of the group responded appreciatively to what they heard and began to empathize with Mary. They realized that it had been easier for them to experience the impact of Lisa's self-destructive behavior than it had been for Mary during her sessions with Lisa because Mary had felt alone in the treatment with the "too-muchness" and had dissociated.

The group then tried to understand what had happened in the previous case conference meeting that had contributed to the change in Mary's work with Lisa. Some group members thought that Mary's empathy for her patient might have increased because she had been able to use the group as a container for her unmetabolized countertransference responses. Other group members wondered whether part of the change was that they were listening differently now: that their ability to understand Mary's approach with Lisa might have increased after they had processed, with the case conference leader's assistance, their reactions.

By the end of the first meeting, the case conference had made a shift from basic assumption group to work group. During most of the initial meeting, the presenter was unable to think or talk directly about her countertransference reactions to Lisa because she was too traumatized. Instead, she unconsciously projected her unbearable feelings into members of the group, who then responded to the presenter's projections either with a sadomasochistic countertransference enactment (criticizing the presenter), an identification with the patient's sadomasochism, or with defenses against participating in such an enactment (silent withdrawal). The group had been operating under the fight/flight basic assumption.

The supervisor provided a containing presence by setting a limit on the sadomasochistic enactment and was able to maintain an analytic attitude toward the case, presenter, and group. The presenter, conference, and eventually the patient benefitted from the experience of the patient's heretofore uncontained dynamics coming into the here-and-now of the case conference and being worked over by the group. (See also Burka et al. [2007] for a discussion of using Bion's theory of container–contained to deepen learning in case conference.)

The Challenges of Working Relationally in Case Conference

Participating in relational psychodynamic case conference can be intimidating not only to group members, but also to group supervisors. All of us have experienced the collapse of thinking that can occur in groups, especially when the group is engaged with affectively loaded material. Primitive states of mind, scapegoating of the presenter, and the disintegration of the group are potential dangers. For this reason, a group supervisor who hopes to take advantage of the power of groups needs to be able to create an environment of sufficient safety and containment of affect so that integration and learning from experience occurs.

In introducing the conference to members, I frame the group as an opportunity for each member to understand something about his or her unique way of listening to, formulating, and responding to clinical material. I request that commentary on the presented material be heard by all as that member's unique associations, rather than advice about how to work with the patient. Of course, no matter how I frame the group task, there is an almost universal pull within case conferences to "supervise" the presenter. An important element of the safety of the group comes from the supervisor intervening if the members of the group try to cope with anxiety or begin to enact dynamics from the case by critiquing the presenter. The supervisor must hold this boundary, as the supervisor did in the example above, for the group to become a sturdy container for emotional material. I also invite group members to bring it to my attention if I become reactive to the presenter.

Psychoanalytic Learning in the Here and Now

Because each member of the case conference has unique areas of emotional intuition and unique points of connection with the clinical material, different aspects of the patient will be spoken to by different members, sometimes leading to differing formulations of the case. Members may also speak from different psychodynamic theoretical perspectives. One role of the case conference is to help individual members gain perspective on the idiosyncrasies and limits of their own convictions about the material. Rather than merely assuming that their associations are "true," members learn about the kinds of dynamics to which they are especially sensitized and the kinds of dynamics to which they can be deaf and blind. They also learn something about the strengths and limitations of their preferred theory. This is a humbling experience for the developing clinician and can motivate self-exploration and the seeking of psychotherapeutic and supervisory help.

Frequently, different members of the group not only hold different aspects of the patient's unconscious, but also (as occurs in a family) hold different aspects of the case conference group's unconscious. If the leader can help the group to tolerate multiple hypotheses about what is going on in the presented treatment, and can also help the group observe and speak to enactments in the group process, valuable psychoanalytic learning takes place. Eventually multiple interpretations that initially seem mutually exclusive may be integrated into a multifaceted understanding of the patient and the therapeutic relationship.

The supervisor in this kind of case conference provides leadership in working analytically with group-generated material. I draw the group's attention to themes that are emerging in the discussion or the way the group members are interacting with one another and raise questions about how these themes and dynamics relate to the case. I may try to integrate multiple case conference members' comments into a coherent formulation and may reference more than one theoretical lens through which one may view the material, saying, for example, "a self psychologist might understand the material this way, whereas a neo-Kleinian would see it that way." I encourage group members to join me in these activities and consider the development of these capacities to be a primary teaching goal of case conference.

CONCLUSION

A relational supervisor tries to adapt her methods to the context in which she is supervising, the needs of her supervisee, and what is being evoked by the particular patient who is under discussion. Although she works from a consistent set of basic principles, the specifics of how those principles translate into technique will differ from one supervisory relationship to the next. In my view, the most effective supervisors have a broad repertoire of methods they can draw upon. One important method is case conference, which lends itself to teaching participants how to work with their subjectivity and emerging unconscious process. Adapting one's method to the specifics of the relational situation is something that every artful clinician learns to do, and this capacity should be a goal in the supervisory situation as well.

In chapter 4, we take a closeup look at a transcript from a supervisory hour. In so doing, we can observe how these methods and techniques and the essential dimensions upon which they are based show up in an actual session.

4

Illustration: An Excerpt From a Transcript of a Supervisory Hour

In this chapter, I use the supervisory session I recorded for the DVD *Relational Psychodynamic Psychotherapy Supervision* (American Psychological Association [APA], 2015; available at http://www.apa.org/pubs/videos/4310942.aspx) to demonstrate some of the features of my supervisory model. I have included a 20-minute excerpt from a transcript of that session. Although it is not necessary to view the full 45-minute video to understand what follows, doing so will enrich the reader's understanding of this material.

THE SUPERVISEE

I had been supervising Jane for about 6 months as an adjunct supervisor at her graduate school training clinic. Jane had requested an additional supervisor, having accumulated several intensive, multiple-year

http://dx.doi.org/10.1037/14802-005
Supervision Essentials for Psychodynamic Psychotherapies, by J. E. Sarnat
Copyright © 2016 by the American Psychological Association.

psychotherapy cases. She was looking for a psychodynamic supervisor who was relationally oriented and asked to work with me.

As is my custom, I had begun by asking Jane what she hoped to gain from our supervision. Jane told me that as her relationships with her patients had deepened, some of those relationships had become quite intense and stressful for her. She wanted to learn more about using her countertransference responses to help her patients. This was our agreed-upon focus, and we arrived at it quite easily. For several months we had been working on the complex termination process that she and her patients were engaged in as Jane prepared to move to a nearby outpatient service to start her internship year.

THE SUPERVISED THERAPY

In this supervision hour, Jane talks to me about her work with Susie, who has a history of multiple abandonments in her early life, as well as physical and emotional abuse. The therapy has been very important to Susie, who has told Jane that their relationship is different from her relationship with the four previous therapists whom she had seen at the same training clinic. Jane, too, has felt that their twice weekly, 2-year treatment has been meaningful, and she is very attached to Susie. Jane has invited Susie to follow her to her internship site when she leaves the clinic, but this would require Susie to travel a longer distance to the sessions and to pay a higher fee. Susie is angry (and, we inferred, hurt) about the disruption in their relationship represented by the additional time and money that Jane's move will require of her. Jane's transition also signifies that Jane is moving ahead with her life, an accomplishment that Susie has been utterly unable to manage herself. Susie—although from a middle-class background and originally on an educational trajectory equivalent to Jane's—has been psychologically stuck for a number of years and unable to complete her education. She is barely making ends meet, working at a low-paying, blue-collar job. Jane and I have wondered how aware Susie may be of Jane's upper-middle-class background, and how much this awareness, along with her awareness that Jane has many capacities that Susie cannot access in herself, may contribute to her feelings of anger and envy. Certainly, Jane contends with feelings of guilt about the differences in their circumstances.

THE SESSION BEFORE THE TRANSCRIPT BEGINS

Jane begins the supervision session by summing up her situation with Susie: "I used to be a very loving, all-loving, idealized object [to Susie], and now there's some real negative transference coming in, which is, I think, positive, but also hard for me to deal with." I hear this statement as Jane's request for help in dealing with Susie's anger about Jane's upcoming move. Jane feels awful about the impending premature termination and is frustrated that Susie is unwilling to discuss the issue.

Jane seems to need me to feel how difficult Susie is being and is candid about her own reactions to Susie's irritable and oppositional mood, a reflection of the safety that Jane feels with me. Describing her feelings toward Susie during the hour, Jane comments, "Sadistic is too strong a word, but . . ." and tells me that she experiences Susie's negativity as a "jab." Jane feels perplexed by Susie's resistance to rescheduling an upcoming therapy hour, which falls on a holiday. She tells me that she cannot imagine why Susie does not think of the potential rescheduled hour as a "nice" part of her day off. I hear Jane's perplexity as a sign of how caught up she is in her countertransference feelings toward Susie because I can well imagine that Susie would experience the offer to reschedule the hour as an inadequate substitute. I also imagine that Susie wouldn't want to let Jane "off the hook" for this cancellation and that she would feel too vulnerable letting Jane know that she even cares about it because the cancellation resonates with Jane's impending departure from the clinic.

The transcript begins a quarter of the way through the 45-minute supervisory session. Although Jane has been listening politely to my formulations and suggestions, she hasn't been able to use them to deepen her feeling or thinking: I am trying to teach, but it isn't clear that I am helping Jane to learn. I want to help Jane to connect to the "little Susie" who can't bear these abandonments, as well as to "adolescent Susie's" maladaptive defenses of oppositional relating and emotional withdrawal. As the excerpt starts, I am searching for how to do this.

THE TRANSCRIPT BEGINS

Jane: What I said was, "I think you're becoming aware, we're both becoming aware, that time is running out and we're not gonna get to everything that you want to talk about." And then I also said, "I seem to bring up things that upset you and then you get angry with me for having brought them up." And I meant the ending. And she agreed with that. And then she switched to how she hates her job and wants to quit her job and the fact that she hates it so much makes her believe that we are gonna end because she has to keep the job to be able to pay. And yet she's told me that she doesn't have enough money to—

Dr. Sarnat: Right. Okay. So let me take us back to the question I raised a minute ago, which is "What's going on with her?" (*Jane:* Yeah.) So we know that she's angry with you, but let's see if we can flesh that out a little bit. (*Jane:* Okay.) I just found that I was remembering something you told me. I think I have the right patient. Is she the one who referred to the backpack?

Jane: Yes.

Dr. Sarnat: Okay. Instead of you having the little Susie in your backpack and taking her where she needs to go, [Susie feels that] you are putting her in this situation where she has to work so hard to get to you. She has to accommodate your schedule. She has to get across the San Rafael Bridge. She has to keep her hard job that she hates.

Jane: Yes. She has to use her healthcare money instead—

Dr. Sarnat: Right. And she's saying, "I hate that I have to be a grown-up and do so much work to keep my relationship to you." (*Jane:* Yes.) "I want to be taken care of." (*Jane:* Yeah.)

Dr. Sarnat: And that backpack image was one of those moments. It comes back to me periodically when I'm trying to listen to you and get back in touch with what's underneath. And I think that that's important not to lose track of. *That's* who you've got in the room: a furious baby who didn't get to be on her mom's back.

Jane: Yes. Yeah.

Dr. Sarnat: Yeah.

Jane: The thing is, what happens—I mean, I think at the very end I say something about, you know, it seems like I wonder if you wish I could just fix this. And she said, "Well, that seems like a reasonable wish to have." And I said, "Of course." But then she gets self-blaming and she says, "But I'm the one that has to fix the ending." And I said, "It doesn't seem fair."

Dr. Sarnat: And that's a lovely intervention. There you are. There you're talking to the little part of her. (*Jane:* Right.) "It doesn't seem fair."

Jane: But the little part of her then hides because she says, "I don't relate to that because—" and I said, "Well, those are *child* feelings." And she said it's not—it's not fair for her to demand that I don't move on when *she's* the one that needs to. Which was very interesting to—

Dr. Sarnat: Say that again. "It's not fair . . . ?"

Jane: It's not fair for her to demand *I* don't move on, as in stay at the clinic or (*Dr. Sarnat:* Mmhmm.) when *she's* the one that needs to. *She* needs to get a job that can afford me.

Dr. Sarnat: So she very quickly goes back to speaking from a sort of "false adult self," I think, defensively—at least that's the way it comes across to me—afraid that you're going to shame her or criticize her or judge her for having these needs and for things looking this way to her, feeling these ways to her, so she anticipates this. This is why Susie's a particularly diffi-cult patient in my view. She's really, really smart and (*Jane:* Yes.) her defen-sive shifts are hard to follow. She's always kind of one step ahead of you, but it's all in the interest of survival.

Jane: Yeah.

Dr. Sarnat: So what is she surviving? What is she protecting herself from there? The possibility that you could feel judgmental of her, toward her, for having these "little" feelings. And I think you have to be very, very careful in the way you address them.

Jane: Okay.

Dr. Sarnat: Not—let me actually ask you this. Let's go back to when you said to her, "Those are child feelings." Or how did you put it? Those are—

Jane: I said like, "But those are your *child* feelings."

Dr. Sarnat: And you were trying to make space for those as you (*Jane:* Yeah.) said that to her? Okay. As if to say, "[of course] all of you isn't adult and rational."

Jane: Right. But she may have not heard it that way.

Dr. Sarnat: Yeah. That's what I'm wondering. That's what I'm wondering. If her experience of your making these demands on her is that it's shameful that she needs any of this, (*Jane:* Yeah.) and so I think that may be why you find yourself in [a struggle with her]—part of why. It would be—anyone would be in a power struggle with her, but part of it, what may make it harder, is that she is so worried that you don't see it from her point of view. That you don't really get it.

Jane: Yeah.

Dr. Sarnat: One way to help her feel you're on her side more—it's very hard to figure out how to be on her side because everything you do, she finds a way to be in this struggle with you.

Jane: Right. She twists it.

Dr. Sarnat: She twists things, yeah. And sometimes you have to just label that when it's happening. But one way [to help her feel you are on her side] is, again, to empathize with what she hates and get her to elaborate on that. (*Jane:* Okay.) Just try to kinda go with it a little more.

Jane: That's interesting because it *bugs* me [when Susie behaves this way], because I think it's a distraction—I either think it's a distraction or I think it's an outsourcing of blame like, "Everything's wrong with the world, and the world just sucks, and what did I ever do to deserve this?"

Dr. Sarnat: Right. But [the idea is] just to find a way to empathize with what she hates and, again, to invite her to explore that. "Tell me more about what you hate. Tell me more about people demanding things from you. What is that like?" In other words, kind of get out of the way.

Jane: But she will go on for—I mean, *[for]ever!* (*Laughs.*)

Dr. Sarnat: So you're afraid that it will be an invitation to externalize if you do that with her.

Jane: Yes, and it feels like a distraction [from] the real problem.

Dr. Sarnat: Tell me about *that*.

Discussion: From Didactic Teaching to Working With Enactment

The pattern of disconnection that I have been describing is apparent in this series of interchanges. I am trying to be helpful, and Jane and I do engage productively with the image of Susie in the backpack as Jane begins to get in touch with more of her patient's unconscious experience. But then I lose Jane again. Despite my efforts to empathize with her situation and to teach her in a nonshaming way, she finds my recommendations unhelpful. When I suggest to Jane that she find a way to "go with" her patient a little more, for example, Jane responds by telling me more about how her patient's behavior "bugs" her.

At this point in the session, I begin to become conscious of feelings of powerlessness and frustration. As I become aware of my reaction, I can interrupt what I have been doing: keeping my feeling of frustration at bay by working harder and harder to "teach" Jane. New possibilities now open up for me. I wonder whether a dynamic that stymied Jane during the clinical hour might be paralleling into our hour and whether Jane could be understood to not only be *telling* me how difficult her patient is, but also (unconsciously) to be *giving me a taste* of what it is like to be with Susie when Susie won't *let* Jane be "on her side." Perhaps this is the relational pattern with which Jane needs my help, a pattern she feels I have not been "getting." Viewing the situation in this way, I can see a way forward. I can demonstrate to Jane, in our relationship, how to work with such reactions. If I can do so, Jane may experience something that is more helpful than my efforts to teach her.

I try several ways to finesse the polite power struggle that Jane and I seem to be engaging in. I stop trying to counter her concerns but instead elaborate upon them, as when I say, "So you are afraid that . . ." Then, when Jane responds to my suggesting she say to Susie, "Tell me more about what you hate," by objecting that Susie will "go on forever" and distract herself from her internal difficulties, I reply, "Tell me about *that*." Here I am modeling, in the here and now, the kind of responsiveness I am hoping Jane can bring in to her work with Susie. The moment feels to me like an energetic turning point in our interaction. The sense of struggle between Jane and me abates as I *demonstrate* welcoming negative feelings simultaneously with *explaining* how to do so.

"Tell me about *that*" was, in part, a strategic move on my part to shift our process. However, it was not *just* a strategic move; it was also an honest expression of my awareness that *I don't actually know* how Jane should work with her patient. If my desire to learn from Jane, as well as to teach her, did not come through to her, I doubt that she would have found my comment as helpful as I believe she did. Still, for the moment, Jane continues to focus on how difficult Susie can be.

Jane: For example, she was talking about how oppressive a certain roommate is, how oppressive a boss is, how terrible our economic political system is. And, you know, I'll say something like, "You are feeling oppressed on every level of your life." And she agrees with that, and I do think it's an avoidance of what's going on internally that's blocking her from, you know, being aware of herself and moving forward and being aware of her feelings and accessing those feelings. Because she can go on and on and spend a whole session talking about how terrible a politician is or her boss.

Dr. Sarnat: Mmhmm, mmhmm. So, have you ever—do you remember a time when she was doing that and you were able to intervene with her in a way that shifted things?

Jane: Well, I've intervened and she's gotten frustrated, I was going to say. There *was* one session fairly recently where she said—she acknowledged, "I know I'm talking about all these things and all these things bug me, but I know—I also know it's an avoidance of what I'm really, you know, what's going on for me emotionally because it's so—there are moments that it—'cause it's so terrifying for me to feel anything emotional. And I know that I'm getting in my own way here."

Dr. Sarnat: Is there a way to refer back to that time?

Jane: Yeah.

Dr. Sarnat: To say, "Is this another one of those moments, like you referred to before, when you wondered if focusing on all of these things was a way *not* to focus on what's inside that's troubling you?" (*Jane:* Yeah.) To ask her, "Is this another one of those? Could this be another one of those moments?" I'm just trying to figure out a way *in* here that she could use.

Jane: You never know. If she's in the right space, she could respond to that. If not, she could feel extremely criticized and pissed off that I've— that now I'm telling her what to talk about. And that I don't believe her, that this stuff is really real to her and important.

Dr. Sarnat: Yeah. Yeah.

Discussion: Mutuality of Power and Authority

In this passage, Jane again politely objects to my technical suggestion: She argues that "going with" Susie's complaints won't work because Susie uses her complaints to avoid awareness of her own feelings. I continue to consult Jane's own expertise, asking, "Do you remember a time when she was doing that and *you* [emphasis added] were able to intervene with her in a way that shifted things?" By acknowledging Jane's expertise, I continue to opt out of our previous struggle.

Jane responds well to this, evoking for the first time in this session an image of Susie when she was not resistant but insightful. I feel cheered by this because I have been trying hard to help Jane to reconnect to her more positive experiences of Susie. The emergence of this memory at this moment could also be understood as a derivative communication to me about Jane's own diminishing experience of resistance in the session.

However, when I return to suggesting an intervention, Jane is equivocal about it, saying it would depend on Susie's mood. Jane clearly is responding less positively to my suggestions than to my drawing out her own ideas. Will my momentary reversion cause the dynamic of struggle and opposition to reappear, or will Jane continue to move closer to Susie and to me?

Jane: She has this very strong—like a child—a very strong need to be believed. (*Dr. Sarnat:* Uh huh.) That was the thing that she said to me early on, when she started expressing how attached she felt to me in contrast to other therapists. She felt like I believed her. (*Dr. Sarnat:* Okay. So, now—) Now that's changed. (*Jane laughs.*)

Dr. Sarnat: Yeah, yeah. And what I hear in the way you described the back-and-forth is that your frustration with her and your judgmental feelings toward her—for the way she defends herself—are part of the—it's a two-person struggle that's going on and she's actualized [the struggle] with you. She's pulled you into a certain kind of interaction with her, which you have gotten into with her. So what you're saying now, it's very touching to me. And I wonder what it would be like to say to her, "Wow, remember when it felt like I believed you and I listened to you and I trusted you? That's really gone, isn't it? We've lost something." What would it be like to say something like that to her?

Jane: She said that before, and so I think me owning that would be great. I think she would respond to that. But what then? What if she says, "Why?" (*Laughs.*)

Discussion: The Dynamic in the Supervisory Relationship Shifts

The earlier struggle between Jane and me does not recur. Instead, Jane brings in two things that are both important and new to the session: her awareness that she and Susie have lost something in their way of interacting and her acknowledgment that Susie has reason, given this change in their interaction, to feel upset. Susie becomes more three-dimensional in Jane's mind; Jane's empathic connection to "little" Susie has increased. In addition, Jane's statement, "I think me owning that would be great. I think she would respond to that," suggests that Jane and I have finally "found" each other—and, together, we have "found" her patient.

Why does this shift in Jane's state of mind happen at this point? Perhaps Jane responded to my being willing to let go of teaching and willing to acknowledge the limits of my own knowledge. Perhaps she felt she had sufficiently gotten across to me how difficult it felt to work with Susie in her current state of mind. Perhaps my processing of my feelings of frustration and powerlessness had affected our interaction for the better. Or perhaps something else shifted in Jane that I cannot know. I do know that *something* shifted because, for the first time in the session, I felt moved; I was touched by Jane's realization that Susie's experience of trust in her had disappeared. Jane laughed nervously in acknowledging this loss, but I felt sad for Jane, as well as for Susie.

As I look back at the sequence now, I wish that I had simply stayed with how touched I felt by this loss, and encouraged Jane to stay with her own feeling rather than focusing on Jane's participation in enactment and her reactivity to Susie. Doing so might have allowed Jane to more fully experience the feelings of loss that had thus far been too much for her to bear. My own anxieties in front of the cameras may have contributed to my feeling pressured to "teach" in this moment, but my reversion to a pattern of intervention that had not been helpful to Jane is not surprising. In my view, in supervision, like in any intimate relationship, dysfunctional interactional patterns often persist and require multiple rounds of working through.

It is also possible that I had another reason for backing off from my experience of being touched at that point. Perhaps I was sensing that it would be too difficult for Jane and for me to stay with painful feelings in front of the cameras, and so I was diluting the power of the moment.

Whatever was going on, the touching moment does not last. I return to teaching mode, and immediately a new anxiety comes up for Jane. As soon as Jane imagines talking with Susie about what had been lost in their relationship, she asks me, "But—what then? What if [Susie] says, 'Why [did I lose my sense of trust in you]?'"

It is interesting to me, as I look back on the session, that *this* is the anxiety that arises in Jane at this moment because I, too, have been feeling under pressure to provide answers. It is possible that she is unconsciously working over one of my problems and identifying with my anxiety. Anxieties flow down the supervisory triad from the supervisor as easily as they flow up from the patient (Gediman & Wolkenfeld, 1980). Of course, Jane also has her own anxieties about knowing enough, and in this moment, it is impossible to be sure exactly who is doing what to whom. In any case, in this next segment, even though I fail to stay with my feelings, I am at least able to be clear that what matters is that Jane prioritize emotional availability with her patient over "knowing the answer."

Dr. Sarnat: Well, but you don't *have* to have the answer to why. What's important is the sadness of that. "Here we are, the situation has changed so radically. We've gotten caught up in a kind of a struggle here. I find myself no longer available to listen in quite the way I was before, and you feel it."

Jane: Yeah.

Dr. Sarnat: "And you hate me for it. You've really lost something." And to be able to just be with the loss in that, which is very much connected with [the fact that] you are now an abandoning figure and there's no way she's gonna feel mostly loving toward you. And then she's triggering some of your own ways you react to somebody who's being entitled and you feel like, "How come you're so entitled?" (*Jane laughs.*) Of course, it's understandable, but I do think that this is one of those moments when stepping out of it and realizing that you are pulled into living out something with her, a struggle, a battle—you know, you're trying to get her to see things a different way—stepping out from that and trying to join with her and say, "It's really hard that we've lost something, that something has really shifted in the way we're being together. I feel it too." You know? (*Jane:* Yeah.) I wonder if that might allow a softening on her part.

Jane: I think so. I think it will ...

Dr. Sarnat: Yeah. So let me just segue for a minute. (*Jane:* Yeah.) What was it like for you, for me to comment on your being pulled into something, that there's this kind of judgmental reaction that you have? I've just now been focusing on something that could be hard to hear. And of course I'm doing it in a very public situation (*Jane:* Yeah. Yeah.) that I know we're both very aware of. So, I just want to check in with you. What is that like?

Jane: Yeah. That's a great question. I think I'm in a place with these patients and maybe with my work in general that I—and in my learning—that I think that that's inevitable and important. (*Dr. Sarnat:* Mmhmm.) And so I—

Dr. Sarnat: You think *what* is inevitable?

Jane: Getting into enactments and then thinking about it and having my own feelings and thinking about what that's saying. And I have such a long relationship with these patients that there's no question—there's a real connection and love there—that I honestly feel it almost makes it stronger for there to be these moments where we have to find our way through whatever's happening, through conflict. I've actually been quite pleased that Susie has started to, you know, present a more—a fuller range of feelings.

Dr. Sarnat: Mm-hmm. Yes, I think it's really progressive for her to be able to hate someone whom she so deeply loves. (*Jane:* Yes.) Yes, and to show you both sides. But, yeah, go ahead.

Jane: But, I was going to say, and in the context of *our* relationship, I know that you know my work and it might feel different if you were somebody that I just met and I'm describing—I've had that happen before—presented at a case conference and had somebody say, "Wow, you just stepped into that one." (*Joint laughter.*) But, it feels totally comfortable to do that with—to go through that with somebody that you trust and knows your work and you feel really known by.

Dr. Sarnat: Yes. In addition to which you have seen *me* step into things with *you* (*Jane:* Exactly. *Laughs.*) and stop and take responsibility for it and then think about it and use it to understand what's going on between us and how that relates to what's going on between you and your patient.

Jane: Right.

Dr. Sarnat: So, I hope that that helps you, too, to feel more accepting of the inevitability of these moments of living something out. Yeah, the living something out is an expression of the depth of your relationship with these patients.

Discussion: Monitoring for Possible Supervisee Injury

During these interchanges, I am aware that I am speaking quite directly to Jane about how she has been triggered, and that I have, in fact, said a number of things over the course of the hour that could be wounding. I therefore interrupt discussion of the session to talk with Jane about our relationship. (I also think that, with the cameras rolling, I may have felt under pressure to illustrate my supervisory model for the viewer.) Jane denies feeling distressed by my observation, and speaks in an apparently shame-free and heartfelt way about how she has come to accept the inevitability of being pulled into enactment. Jane's comfort is an indication of her maturity as a relationally oriented psychodynamic psychotherapist, as well as her confidence in her own capacities and her trust that I respect her work. I never assume, however, that a supervisee's expressed comfort is the whole story. I continue to monitor the relationship for signs that the supervisee may feel criticized, shamed, or inadequate and would work with those feelings, which interfere with learning and emotional development, if they did appear. I would also take into account my own contribution to whatever difficulties developed between us.

In this session I acknowledge my own vulnerability to "stepping into things." I am referring here to an enactment that I had precipitated in the days before the filming. It seems important to include a description of that enactment here, although it requires us to leave the session for a moment.

A PRESESSION SUPERVISOR-INITIATED ENACTMENT

As part of our preparation for the filming, Jane wrote up a statement about her work with Susie, and I wrote up a statement about my work with Jane; both statements were to be submitted to the film producer. I ran my statement by Jane first for comment, as I always do about anything I write about our work. Jane was offended by my write-up. She felt that I had made her sound like she had more countertransference problems and was less skillful than she thought was actually true.

After thinking about her feedback, I realized that it resonated, at least in part. I acknowledged that to Jane and shared some of my thoughts about why my summary might have come across that way. I told Jane that I had become aware of my resistance to being in touch with my feelings of anxiety about the upcoming filming and that my need to ward off my own anxiety might have caused me to be out of touch with hers. I also thought that the tone of my write-up might have expressed an unconscious effort to project my own anxieties into her. I let her know that I felt sorry to have used her (unconsciously) in this way, especially at a moment when she, too, was feeling so vulnerable.

Having owned my own contribution, I invited Jane to think, as well, about the ways in which the intensity of her response to my write-up might express *her* anxieties—anxieties about the filming, anxieties about my view of her, and anxieties deriving from her relationships with her patients as she prepared to leave them. She agreed that at that stressful moment, she might have been especially vulnerable to seeing negative implications in my write-up. I commented that it seemed understandable that the issue of exposing vulnerability would be a mutual flashpoint in our relationship at such a moment. I also suggested that our experience with this toxic cocktail of intersubjectively convergent anxieties could help us both to empathize with her patients during this difficult time. Jane found these thoughts helpful, and the tension between us dissipated.

RETURNING TO THE TRANSCRIPT

As the supervision session proceeds, I talk to Jane again about working her way out of the enactment in which she has been caught with Susie.

Dr. Sarnat: And finding a way to work with it, though. Not to just stay in it but to work with it. And to say to Susie, "I almost feel like we're—we've lost—in a way, we've lost each other already." (*Jane:* Hmmm.) "Our last session isn't for a few weeks, but something of what we had feels like it's not here right now." (*Jane:* Yeah.) "We've lost touch with it." That's a way to bring the ending in that's connected with where she actually *is*, which is out of touch with her loving feelings for you and her need for you.

Jane: Not always. I mean, she will show—in that moment, she will bring it back. I just had the thought if I were to say that to her, she would probably say, "*You're* the one that thinks we're having problems here. I don't think we're having any issues here."

Dr. Sarnat: Okay, well I would stick with it. If she said that—let's play this out a little more. (*Jane:* Yeah.) If she said that to me in that situation, I imagine—of course I'm not in the room with her so this is me imagining a Susie—and it's also being *me* in the room, not *you* in the room. So, with those two caveats, if she said to me, "I don't think we're having any problems," I would say, "Well, *I* do, though. *I* feel a loss. *I* think that—it feels to me like we're in a kind of a struggle, and I know how angry you are and how difficult this is that *you* have to accommodate to my schedule and *you* have to schlep across the bridge to see *me*, and *you* have to work at your difficult job to make it possible to see me. I know how hard that is and I think it's understandable that things don't feel so easy between us right now."

Discussion: Supervisor Persistence as Hindrance and/or Help

During this session, I point out to Jane multiple times that she is caught in an enactment. I bring it up again here, continuing to suggest sample interventions. How to understand my doggedness? Is this an expression of a need to be The One Who Knows? Or a giving-in to superego pressure to do everything possible on the patient's behalf? Possibly both. At the same time, persistence can be a valuable supervisory quality when a supervisee is struggling to take in a new way of working that is emotionally challenging. From this perspective, Jane is experimenting with a new way of thinking about her patient and then enlisting my help in resolving each of the anxieties and difficulties that emerge for her when she imagines taking this approach. I lean toward interpreting my persistence in this more positive way because, although there is an apparent similarity in our interaction here to our interaction earlier in the session, when I was working too hard to "teach" Jane, my experience during this part of the session is different. Now, I feel there is a creative back and forth between us, and the interaction seems more engaged on Jane's part.

My persistence with Jane may also help her to learn something about how to be clinically persistent with her patient. Interestingly, my recommendation to Jane in response to one of her questions in this passage is to "be persistent," and so the medium matches the message.

AFTER THE TRANSCRIPT: THE FINAL MINUTES OF THE SESSION

Although our excerpt from the transcript ends here, two things happened during the final 12 minutes of the session that I feel are important to mention. First, Jane raised a worry about maintaining her sense of conviction about the value of her work with Susie in the face of Susie's devaluation of her and the therapy. I suggested that Jane might remind herself about how I see the therapy at those moments. I am giving Jane something to "take with her" as we approach the end of the hour. In retrospect, I think my comment was a way for me to address *both* of our anxieties about the impending end of the session because separation anxiety was a dynamic that was being activated in both the clinical and supervisory relationships.

Second, it is worth noting that in these last few minutes of the session, I referred to a "parental couple," a term traditionally used among psychoanalytic practitioners to refer to the archetypal image a child carries of mother and father. Of course this term reflects a dyad-normative concept of the family (Chang, 2015), a concept that is both limiting and prejudicial, and implicitly a hetero-normative concept as well. Hearing myself, I realized that I did not want to let the bias implicit in this terminology go unqualified. I therefore went on to speak, more generically, of a "caregiver" who is supported by "a spouse—or whatever support that caregiver would have." (See chap. 6 for more on working with difference.)

AFTERWARD

Jane's countertransference challenge with Susie is far from resolved at the end of this excerpt. But, in my view, it is through the cumulative impact of experiences of this kind, over time, that a supervisee develops complex capacities and skills. And, in fact, in the sessions immediately following this one, Jane found herself more able to hold the "little" Susie in mind, was less caught up in angry feelings toward Susie, and could better see the ways in which she had been playing into the struggle that had developed between them.

Susie responded to this shift in Jane. She made the transition to the new clinic, although she did need to reduce her weekly sessions from two to one. She was unhappy, of course, about how difficult it was to get there and actually used part of her first session at the new clinic to call so that Jane would talk her through finding the place in real time. Both Jane and I found this unwitting display of vulnerability and dependence touching.

When Jane told Susie about a free shuttle bus that connected public transit to the clinic, Susie was amazed and delighted. After using the shuttle for the first time, she described to Jane, in an almost childlike way, how nice the driver was, and all the details of how terrific riding the shuttle was. When Jane recounted this to me, we couldn't help but think of "little" Susie, finally getting a ride in the backpack after all.

CONCLUSION

I conclude by explaining how I think this supervisory session illustrates the three essential dimensions of the relational model of psychodynamic supervision. These dimensions are: the supervisor's authority, focus, and mode of intervention.

Authority Relations

The relationship Jane and I have of "mutuality in the context of asymmetry" comes through in this excerpt. Because I had previously let Jane know that I understood that both of us were vulnerable to enactment and unconscious defensiveness, Jane feels free to tell me about, and even to show me, her countertransference reactivity. I feel authorized to work directly with Jane's countertransference issue, even though doing so might provoke anxiety in her, because we had explicitly negotiated this as a focus for our supervisory work. My willingness to acknowledge what I do not know, as well as my (implicit) acceptance of the limitations of my initial efforts to help, make possible the progress that occurs in the second part of the excerpt. Also, because I am mindful that I have more power than does Jane, I take responsibility for checking in with her about the impact of my confrontations, rather than depending upon her to bring up such feelings herself. Finally, I think carefully about my own possible contributions to Jane's anxieties and work to identify, understand, and take responsibility for enactments that I introduce into our relationship.

A Focus That Includes the Supervisory Relationship and Nonsemantic Material

Attentiveness to what is going on in the supervisory relationship and comfort with working directly in that relationship lie at the heart of the relational model. Disconnection in the supervisory relationship—that one is failing to get through to one's supervisee—is an example of the kind of dynamic to which a relational supervisor pays attention. During a period of disconnection, a supervisor can, as I did in this transcript, offer clinical "wisdom" that is useless to the supervisee, even though the supervisee may not indicate so because of "politeness," a lack of confidence in her own experience, or enactment of a parallel process from the therapy.

In this session, I start out in didactic mode but then notice that something is amiss: that I am working very hard but that Jane seems not to be taking in my point of view. I then shift my focus to what is going on in the here and now with Jane, opening to my actual experience. The nonsemantic aspects of our interaction—Jane's involvement or lack of involvement in what I am trying to teach, the subtle element of resistance, and finally the emerging sadness about the change in Jane's relationship with Susie—are as important to this supervisory hour as Jane's report of what was said in the presented session.

A Mode of Intervention That Draws Upon Clinical Expertise

In this excerpt, as I begin to "find" Jane, our relationship becomes a vehicle for experiential learning. I draw upon my clinical expertise and begin to metabolize a disturbance that seems to have paralleled from the therapeutic relationship into the supervisory relationship, working in the here and now with an unprocessed state of resistance and disconnection that originates in the clinical relationship and gets traction in the supervisory relationship. As I work with that state in our relationship, Jane has the opportunity to experience for herself something of what Susie needs to experience with her and can carry that experience back into the session with Susie.

How a Relational Model Is Different—and Not Different

Throughout the session, there are ways in which my approach is no different from that of a nonrelational psychodynamic supervisor. I offer formulations, suggest interventions, and explain psychoanalytic concepts. I also do a fair amount of empathizing and normalizing of my supervisee's reactions, something that good supervisors of every persuasion do. Even in this excerpt, which I selected to demonstrate what is different about my approach, the areas of similarity are clear. What makes this approach different is that in addition to all of the above activities, I pay attention to the supervisory relationship and focus on it as an important source of information and a means to facilitate supervisee development. A supervisor's sensitivity to moments of connection and disconnection, to enactment within the supervisory dyad, and to the presence or absence of mutuality in the supervisory relationship is key. The relational model normalizes, provides a theoretical context for, and creates a frame for working in this way.

5

Common Supervisory Issues, Part I: Working With Supervisee "Difficulties"

This chapter and the two that follow address common issues that arise in supervision. In this chapter, I explore how a relational supervisor works with the difficulties that supervisees bring.

Difficulties can and do emerge at any stage in the life cycle of the psychotherapist. The focus of this series is primarily on supervising psychotherapists in training. Therefore, most of this chapter pertains to supervisees who are in Phases 2 and 3 of psychotherapist development, as defined by the model of Rønnestad and Skovholt (2003); that is, they are in the Beginning Student Phase or the Advanced Student Phase. I also describe my work with one consultee (that is, a licensed clinician who voluntarily sought my help) who was in Phase 5, The Experienced Professional Phase.

For simplicity, in this chapter I focus primarily on the intrapsychic component of supervisee difficulties; this allows me to create categories to

http://dx.doi.org/10.1037/14802-006
Supervision Essentials for Psychodynamic Psychotherapies, by J. E. Sarnat

differentiate different levels of supervisee difficulty. However, it is important to remember that the reality is more complex; difficulties are experienced in interaction with particular patients and supervisors; a relational model of supervision takes into account that difficulties always include an intersubjective element.

From an intrapsychic point of view, a continuum of degree of supervisee difficulty may be defined. At one end of that continuum, we find basically competent and emotionally healthy supervisees who periodically run up against their own personalities as they engage with patients and supervisors. The relational supervisor frames the emergence of such ordinary supervisee personality issues in terms of *regression in the service of growth and learning*. In the middle of the continuum are the supervisees with moderate difficulties. Such supervisees are either going through a stressful life event, which impairs their availability to provide care for the patient, or find themselves trapped within a particularly challenging transference/countertransference constellation, which they can't work their way out of without sustained, good-enough supervisory help. At the far end of the continuum are the supervisees whose internal problems are so severe and chronic that they impede their work with patients or supervisors, or both, in an ongoing way. This level of difficulty, by definition, cannot be fully addressed in supervision, even with a supervisor who adapts optimally to his supervisee's needs over a period of time.

ORDINARY DIFFICULTIES: REGRESSION IN THE SERVICE OF LEARNING

Racker (1957), in an effort to give analysts permission to acknowledge their inevitable psychological limitations, observed that, "we are still children and neurotics even when we are adults and analysts" (p. 307). His comment applies to patients, clinicians, and supervisors alike. When a relational supervisor creates sufficient safety in supervision, the supervisee is freed to show his childlike and conflicted parts—and to get help with these, rather than feeling the need to present a false professional self (Eckler-Hart, 1987). During such moments, one might say that the supervisee has *regressed in the service of learning* (Frawley-O'Dea & Sarnat, 2001;

Sarnat, 1998). Regression in the service of learning is a concept that is closely related to Ernst Kris's (1936) more general ego-psychological concept of *regression in the service of the ego.*

My colleague and I (Frawley-O'Dea & Sarnat, 2001) used the term *regression* to capture the kinds of experiences that most supervisees—and supervisors—are not used to acknowledging in the context of their professional roles. These include

> ... regression from secondary process to primary process, regression from reality to fantasy, regression from more complex and mature modes of thinking and feeling to more primitive modes of thinking and feeling, regression from more organized self states to more primitive self states, and regression from more mature relational patterns to more infantile modes of relationship. (p. 107)

We borrowed Aron and Bushra's (1998) view of regression in the service of learning as "a way of accessing and reconnecting with blocked off aspects of the imaginal and experiential dimension of life" (p. 390). Similar to what a patient may experience with a psychotherapist, it is a state of mind in which a supervisee temporarily delegates to the supervisor his self-observing function. Delegating one's observing ego to another allows an experience of creative disorganization that can be utilized for growth. Similar to the process that transpires between caregiver and infant, when the supervisor contains her supervisee's regressive experiences in the supervisory hour, the dyad enters into a mutual regulation pattern that fosters development (Beebe & Lachmann, 1988; Stern, 1985). (For more on this topic, see Sarnat [1998], and chap. 6 in Frawley-O'Dea & Sarnat [2001].)

How does the supervisor facilitate a generative learning regression, one that permits disorganization and growth but is also sufficiently contained so that the learning task remains front and center? She creates a supervisory environment that is attuned not only to the supervisee's growing edges, but also to the supervisee's narcissistic vulnerabilities and other anxieties, an environment that is minimally shaming because of the supervisor's willingness to consider her own part in difficulties that arise (Frawley-O'Dea & Sarnat, 2001).

Regression in the Service of Learning: An Example

My session with Jane, which is described in chapter 4, provides an example of regression in the service of learning. During much of the transcribed supervision session, this able and mature graduate student is caught up in a reactive response to her patient. She complains about how difficult her patient is, wants me to join with her in seeing her patient as the problem, and for a period of time, seems unable to step back and think about what may be going on unconsciously with her patient, even when I directly ask her to do so. Here Jane was taking the risk of regressing in supervision in order to learn. She commented to me subsequently that, during the transcribed hour, she had the sense that a part of her self was actively *choosing* to "lean in" to her feelings of frustration with her patient. By doing so, she unwittingly induced in me a direct experience of the difficulty with which she had been struggling unsuccessfully with her patient. I got a taste of what she had been going through when virtually all of her comments to her patient in recent hours had either fallen flat or been actively rejected. I believe that Jane was unconsciously introducing this difficult experience into her relationship with me so that we might work on those feelings together.

The didactic and patient-centered approach with which I had started the session—explaining the patient to Jane and suggesting to her how to work with the patient—did not prove a good match for Jane in this (regressed) state of mind. When I let go of the idea that I could help Jane through instruction, I could draw upon my clinical knowledge of how to work with such moments in the here and now. I said to myself, "*I need to pay attention to my own feelings, think about what may be going on unconsciously between us, and figure out what else I can do (or not do) to move our process forward.*" I started to open myself to the regression that Jane was bringing into the here and now of our relationship. Almost immediately, our interaction shifted and Jane had a new experience that taught her something about working with her patient's frustrating responses and ultimately led to her appreciating her participation in cocreating their frustrating interaction pattern. (See chap. 4 for more on how this played out.)

MODERATE SUPERVISEE DIFFICULTIES

To illustrate working with a moderate, but still workable, level of supervisee difficulty, I offer two examples. The first describes a supervisee in personal crisis. The second describes a supervisee with an inhibition that affected her relationships with many patients.

Example 1: A Supervisee in Personal Crisis

Katherine[1] was an experienced professional who had fine capacities, excellent training, a good deal of clinical experience. She was currently in her own intensive psychotherapy. Temporarily impaired by acute grief, she came to me for consultation. She was having trouble thinking clearly and was feeling overwhelmed by her relationship with a patient with a psychotic transference. Her difficulties showed up in consultation not only in the feelings of helplessness, fear, and persecution that she described experiencing with her patient, but also in her confused thinking as she presented her patient to me and in my own feelings of disorientation and anxiety in response.

Katherine started off the supervisory session by tearfully describing an encounter that she had just had with a friend. I listened sympathetically to her story, offering her the time and space that she needed to cry. After a few minutes, Katherine calmed down, and we were able to turn, quite naturally, to her case. However, Katherine presented in a way that I found chaotic and hard to follow. Although I felt anxious about the degree of her disorganization and thought it might reflect her enmeshment in a psychotic transference-countertransference, I elected not to bring it up with her at this point, sensing that doing so would only further overwhelm her, burdening her rather than containing (Bion, 1962) her. This initial period of adaptation to Katherine's regression paid off. Over the course of the session, Katherine eventually regained her capacity to think, accurately observing herself and her patient. By the end of the session, I could talk to her about my thoughts about what was going on in the therapy, and she could take it in.

---

[1]A transcript of the consultation with Katherine can be found in chapter 6 of *The Supervisory Relationship* (Frawley-O'Dea & Sarnat, 2001).

Here the medium of supervision matched my message. The content we discussed—how to help the patient to calm down and reclaim her mind—was directly parallel to what Katherine had just experienced with me. I was not only helping my supervisee to think; I was also, simultaneously, providing her with a model for how to work with her patient's regression.

Example 2: A Workable Supervisee Personality Problem

Supervisees encounter difficulties when their own personality issues overlap with those of their patient. Elkind (1992) describes this common clinical phenomenon as an intersubjective process of "interlocking vulnerabilities." But some supervisees have more difficulty than do others in letting go of a dysfunctional pattern that they are enacting with patients. When a supervisee struggles with the same difficulties in working with more than one patient, it is reasonable to assume that a good piece of the problem is due to the supervisee's chronic defensive patterns. Sometimes these difficulties can be worked through, at least to some degree, in supervision if the supervisor is available to engage experientially when the problem manifests in the supervisory relationship and to consider how her own interlocking vulnerability also may be in play.

In my first paper on supervision (Sarnat, 1992), I described my work with a supervisee who had difficulty asserting herself with many of her patients. The problem appeared most clearly in negotiating and collecting fees. My strenuous efforts to teach her how to be more effective around fee setting and collecting went nowhere. In fact, she eventually reacted by feeling "pushed around" by me as I persisted in talking to her about the problem. My own interlocking vulnerability caused me to put too much pressure on her. I became dominating, and she began submitting to me in a manner similar to how she submitted to her patients. But then, this submissive supervisee started "pushing around" some of her patients—becoming impatient with them, perhaps in identification with how I had become impatient with her. Her frustration built as she realized that, under my "watch," things were getting worse in her treatments rather than better. Finally, she blew up at me—a turning point in the supervision. She wanted me off her back! My nondefensive and nonretaliatory response to her outburst seemed to free her—much as can happen in psychotherapy—and allowed her to become less guilty about and fearful of her aggressive feelings. She began to use them more consciously in her work, instead of stifling them. Suddenly, she felt freer to address fee issues with her patients.

It is important to note, in respecting the "teach–treat" boundary, that the goal here was a limited supervisory one rather than a more general psychotherapeutic one: to help my supervisee overcome her inhibition in confronting patients. Supervisees often are able to use supervision to overcome problems in their role as psychotherapist well before they can do so in their relationships with significant others.

Of course, from a relational perspective, when supervisees do not succeed in overcoming their difficulties in supervision, one must wonder to what degree that failure results from the contribution of an unrecognized difficulty of the supervisor. Initially, my own difficulty made things worse for my supervisee. If I had become defensive or retaliatory when she got furious with me, my supervisee might not have overcome her inhibition, and that would not necessarily be because her problem was too entrenched. Resolving such issues requires a supervisee and a supervisor to work well together. For this reason, seeking consultation can be of enormous benefit to supervisors who are stuck in something with a supervisee. (See chap. 8 for more about the importance of consultation.)

WHEN SUPERVISEE PROBLEMS ARE MORE SEVERE

When supervisees have difficulties that improve very little or not at all, even with excellent supervisory help, these difficulties are "serious." Falender and Shafranske (2004) observed that a supervisor who finds herself in this situation should make sure to take a series of specific steps, including defining clear expectations, offering feedback about the problematic behavior, seeking consultation, and documenting efforts to remediate the problem and the problem's persistence or resolution. These steps are necessary not only because they are good pedagogy, but also to assure that the supervisee receives due process. Of course, a great deal is at stake. As the *Guidelines for Clinical Supervision in Health Service Psychology* (American Psychological Association [APA], 2014) state, "supervisees who are determined to lack sufficient foundational or functional competencies for entry to the profession may be terminated to protect potential recipients of the supervisee's practice" (p. 26).

Every supervisor hopes that effective intervention will make "termination" of their supervisee unnecessary. Remediation offered to trainees with serious difficulties often extends beyond the supervision itself: referrals to personal psychotherapy, additional supervision, and/or additional course work (Falender & Shafranske, 2004). In some training settings, there is also the option for cotherapy or close monitoring of supervisee performance via videotaping, both to keep track of the supervisee's progress and to assure that patients receive competent treatment.

But what can a relational supervisor do within the supervisory relationship itself? Two examples allow us to explore this question. The first, published by Ladany, Friedlander, and Nelson (2005), provides an opportunity to elucidate the ways in which a relational approach to working with a supervisee's serious difficulties would be similar to and different from other approaches. The second example shows a relational approach to what turns out to be an unresolvable (at least for that supervisory dyad) supervisee difficulty (Frawley-O'Dea & Sarnat, 2001).

Example 1: A Serious Supervisee Difficulty Affects Her Patients

Ladany et al. (2005) published a transcript of a supervision hour with Sarah, a supervisee who experienced serious problems. Sarah repeatedly expressed angry feelings about mothers to her supervisor, and she found reasons to avoid engaging with mothers in family sessions. Sarah starts the supervisory hour in denial of her problem and is defensive and prickly in her interaction with her supervisor. Ladany and colleagues call the example a "successfully resolved problematic behavior event" because some progress is made in the course of the presented supervisory hour. Although this is clearly the case, this supervisee's serious difficulties are only partially resolved by the end of the presented supervisory hour.

The supervisor intervenes with Sarah in a number of ways that are in keeping with how a relational psychodynamic supervisor might intervene: He makes use of his clinical skills for educational purposes, is attentive to the supervisory relationship, normalizes Sarah's difficulties, and acknowl-edges and works with aspects of his supervisory countertransference. In addition, in describing his process, this supervisor uses terms such as "regression," "defense," "supervisory alliance," and "countertransference," showing that the supervisor is comfortable with psychodynamic thinking.

Yet there is at least one important difference between how this super-visor worked with Sarah and how I imagine I might work with her, based on the limited information provided. When Sarah, in tears, says, "I just can't do this [supervisory] conversation," her supervisor suggests that Sarah "take a break" and return in 20 minutes. This I would not do. I agree with the author that the supervisor should not try to work through Sarah's anger toward her mother in supervision, and also that Sarah's intense level of emotional arousal would interfere with her capacity to learn in the session. But neither of these points requires the supervisee to interrupt the supervision session. I would instead try to help Sarah to calm down during the supervisory hour while refraining from additional exploration of her early relationship history. This supervisor saw introducing the break as a way to minimize his super-visee's regression, but Sarah's regression was already fully represented in the supervisory hour in her upset and tears. Given this, the question is whether Sarah could benefit more (in terms of her development as a psychothera-pist) from her supervisor communicating comfort with and a desire to help her with her regression, or from asking her to handle it on her own.

In explaining why he initiated the break, this supervisor also expressed concern that he might shame Sarah if he started to work with her emotions and then had to later set a limit on doing so. Although I do not know Sarah, and she might have been a particularly challenging supervisee, I have had the experience of making space for other supervisees' intense feelings and find-ing that their feelings resolve sufficiently after a few minutes so that we can shift our focus to working with the patient. (See the example of Katherine in this chapter.) If, after helping a supervisee with his upset, he expected more "therapeutic" interaction, and if my limiting that interaction evoked feelings of shame in him, I would hope that we could work with those feelings as well.

Actually, it seems to me that suggesting a break might have been sham-ing to Sarah in itself because the supervisor could be understood to be say-ing, "Your feelings are too much for me." Moreover, when Sarah returned after the break, and the supervisor greeted her with "Feeling better?" Sarah replied, "Yeah. Sorry. I'll try not to do that again" (p. 202). The supervisor infers from this that Sarah felt that expressing her emotions was bad, and he tries to reassure her by saying, "Hey, your reactions are real, and real is a good thing" (p. 202). However, in my view, the supervisor's verbal reassurance could not undo the nonverbal message he had communicated by initiating the break: his discomfort with the intensity of her feelings. The supervisor's way of interacting is, in this way, process inconsistent with what the supervisor is presumably trying to teach Sarah about working with people who stir up strong feelings in her. If a supervisor, instead, contained Sarah's feelings, one would hope that the experience, over time, would help her to develop the capacity to regulate her own affects better and provide the same affect regulation to her patients—even those patients who evoked strong negative feelings in her, like mothers in families.

Of course, it is important to consider that this supervisor—who actually knew Sarah, rather than needing to imagine her, as I have done—might have had reason to think that she couldn't have made use of the kind of process I am envisioning here. Perhaps her supervisor knew her to be too brittle, based on previous encounters in supervision. It is also important to remember that the work this supervisory pair actually *did* was helpful: By the end of the supervisory session, they had arrived at a shared understanding of Sarah's problem and had agreed upon a plan for moving forward. I am left wondering, however, if Sarah was ultimately able to resolve her serious difficulties sufficiently to meet her supervisor's and her training program's expectations for competent and ethical practice.

Example 2: A Serious Supervisee Difficulty Affects the Supervisory Relationship

What happens when, after working hard with a supervisee on a conflictual supervisory relationship, no progress is made? This difficult situation was described in a vignette in *The Supervisory Relationship* (Frawley-O'Dea & Sarnat, 2001).

Early in supervision, Bernie developed intensely negative feelings toward Carolyn, his supervisor, telling Carolyn that she was interested in neither him nor the supervised case—that she was "'dead—bored and boring'" (p. 164). Carolyn acknowledged that Bernie had picked up on something real and that she would like to understand and change the situation by exploring together what was going on. Did Bernie have any thoughts about what this experience might mean in terms of either the supervision or the supervised treatment? For instance, was "boredom and deadness" a state he experienced with the patient? Bernie became furious and accused Carolyn of blaming him for her problem. Carolyn was taken aback. Although she acknowledged that her first question had focused away from her own possible contribution to the problem, Bernie's fury did not resolve.

In the next session, Bernie apologized, explaining that his reactivity was related to a dynamic he realized he had not worked through in his previous personal treatment. Bernie asked to continue to work with the dynamic in supervision; Carolyn agreed to give it a try. He then told her about his relationship with his mother, who had been sick throughout his childhood and who died when he was an adolescent.

For 8 weeks, they tried to work with Bernie's negative transference to Carolyn. However, despite his growing intellectual understanding of its origins, Bernie's reactivity continued, and it was impossible to focus sufficiently on Bernie's patients. Carolyn finally told Bernie that he would need to take the issue to a psychotherapist and focus on the patient during their supervision. She assured him that many clinicians, herself included, returned to treatment when previously unaddressed issues became salient for them. Bernie understood that supervision could not go on as it had, but he did not feel ready to return to treatment. Exhausted by dealing with these feelings, he decided to take a leave of absence from his training program to try to figure out what to do next. The supervision came to a sad and premature end.

This supervisor's efforts to work with her supervisee's serious difficulty failed, and as I look again at this vignette, I find that I have several concerns about how the supervisor handled the problem. Eight weeks is a long time to try to work on a dysfunctional supervisory relationship; during that period the needs of Bernie's patients were sidelined, raising ethical issues.[2]

---

[2]See *Guidelines for Clinical Supervision in Health Service Psychology* (APA, 2014): "Supervisors uphold their primary ethical and legal obligation to protect the welfare of the client/patient" (p. 26).

(For further discussion of the ethical challenges of balancing patient and supervisee needs in supervision, see chap. 7.) It is also important for a supervisor to seek consultation in such situations, to sort through and try to resolve whatever she may be contributing to the difficulty, and I do not know whether consultation was sought in this situation. In addition, when the supervisee's primary issue is with a supervisor, and the supervisor is unable to resolve the issue, the supervisor and training program should consider whether the problem may be one of supervisory match. A training program's willingness to authorize one "no fault" transfer to a different supervisor when an unresolvable issue comes up for a supervisee can reduce supervisee shame and sometimes resolve the dilemma. If problems arise with a second supervisor, it is clear to all concerned that a serious supervisee difficulty is involved and must be addressed.

However, something important did happen as a result of the 8 weeks of supervisory work: Bernie came to accept that he needed to either return to personal treatment or reconsider training in this field. Helping a supervisee reach such a conclusion for himself is always an accomplishment.

CONCLUSION

The relational psychodynamic approach to working with ordinary and moderate supervisee difficulties is to treat them as opportunities for learning and growth. The supervisor adapts as fully as she can, without sacrificing the patient's needs or the standards of the program in which the supervisee is enrolled. The concept of regression in the service of learning is helpful in that regard, and the relational model provides theory that supports the supervisor at moments of crisis or intense affect in the supervisory hour. The supervisor also strives to be mindful of her own contribution to difficulties that develop.

Working with serious supervisee difficulties is a different matter. When such difficulties do not resolve, it becomes important to seek consultation from others, consider issues of supervisee/supervisor match, and keep in mind the best interest of the patient along with the best interest of the supervisee.

6

Common Supervisory Issues, Part II: Working With Difference

This chapter shows how the relational perspective sharpens the lens through which a supervisor views issues of difference in the supervisory and psychotherapeutic relationships. The relational perspective is helpful in facilitating the process of acknowledging difference, sensitizing supervisors to the complex issues involved, and supporting the emotional work required to address those issues.

The topic of diversity has received significant attention in professional psychology in recent years. In 2003, The American Psychological Association (APA) published *Guidelines on Multicultural Education, Training, Research, Practice, and Organizational Change for Psychologists*. In addition, "diversity" is the second "domain" listed in the *Guidelines for Clinical Supervision in Health Service Psychology* (APA, 2014). During these years, difference has also become a topic of interest in the relational psychoanalytic literature. When we were writing our book (Frawley-O'Dea & Sarnat, 2001), psychoanalytic theorizing of this area had hardly begun,

http://dx.doi.org/10.1037/14802-007
Supervision Essentials for Psychodynamic Psychotherapies, by J. E. Sarnat
Copyright © 2016 by the American Psychological Association.

and we did not address the topic of difference per se.[1] As I write now, 15 years later, such an omission is unthinkable.

I begin this chapter by indicating some ways in which the relational model supports the development of multicultural supervisor competencies that are defined in the counseling psychology literature. Then, I look at how the relational psychoanalytic literature deepens a supervisor's understanding of working with difference. Finally, I discuss an extended vignette from that literature to illustrate the ideas presented.

HOW THE RELATIONAL MODEL OF PSYCHODYNAMIC SUPERVISION SUPPORTS COUNSELING PSYCHOLOGY'S MULTICULTURAL COMPETENCIES

What are the points of intersection between the counseling psychology literature on supervisor multicultural competency and the relational model of psychodynamic supervision? To begin, they share a basic premise: Counseling psychology assumes that cultural difference is a phenomenon that needs to be recognized in every interpersonal encounter (Bernard & Goodyear, 2014); the relational model of psychodynamic supervision emphasizes adapting supervisory technique to each person's ("cultural") uniqueness. In addition, a relational supervisor pays attention to what she introduces into the supervisory relationship and takes responsibility for initiating necessary conversations in supervision, even when emotions run high. The model is thus well-suited to developing two supervisor multicultural competencies that are emphasized in the counseling psychology literature: developing supervisor self-awareness and opening conversations about difference.

Developing Supervisor Self-Awareness

Supervisor self-awareness is emphasized repeatedly in the counseling psychology literature on supervisor multicultural competence. Ancis and Ladany (2001) identified five domains of supervisor competency that they viewed as

---

[1]We did, however, address the more limited topic of gender and sexism (see Frawley-O'Dea & Sarnat [2001], chapter 5).

necessary for facilitating supervisee growth in working with "multicultural" issues: supervisor-focused personal development, supervisee-focused development, skills and interventions, process, and outcome evaluation. Of these five, three of the domains call for self-awareness and awareness of relationship: supervisor-focused personal development, supervisee-focused personal development, and process. Ancis and Ladany (2001, 2010) also offered to supervisors, through their heuristic model of nonoppressive interpersonal development (HMNID), "a model for understanding patterns of thoughts, feelings, and behaviors about themselves, their trainees, and clients across specific demographic variables (i.e., race, ethnicity, sexual orientation, gender, disability, socioeconomic status)" (2001, p. 63). This well-elaborated model is intended to facilitate supervisor self-awareness. *The Guidelines for Clinical Supervision in Health Service Psychology* (APA, 2014) reconfirmed supervisor self-awareness as a multicultural imperative, asserting, "Supervisors [should] strive to develop and maintain self-awareness regarding their diversity competence" (p. 15). In breaking down this supervisor self-awareness into its components, the guidelines emphasized supervisor self-reflection, stating that it leads to ongoing supervisor growth, models this capacity for the supervisee, and contributes to an environment of safety in supervision.

Falender and Shafranske (2004), too, emphasized cultural self-awareness as a critical precondition to awareness of cultural factors in relationships with others: "Until a supervisor has developed this level of competency, it is difficult, if not impossible, to be an excellent supervisor" (p. 122). They noted, however, the failure of most training programs to promote sufficient self-exploration in either psychotherapists or supervisors. The relational model of psychodynamic supervision, with its emphasis on self-awareness and self-reflection, can be useful in addressing this failure.

The Challenge of Talking About Difference

According to Ladany, Friedlander, and Nelson (2005), learning how to open conversations around difference is a crucial supervisory competency:

> Supervisors, like therapists (Thompson and Jenal, 1994), need to initiate difficult discussions of cultural similarities and differences.

Supervisees' biases are more likely to be revealed and worked through when the atmosphere encourages these types of important discussions. (p. 59)

Bernard and Goodyear (2014) concurred: "We now have evidence that if supervisors do not initiate discussions about culture in supervision, very few discussions occur (Duane & Roehlk, 2001; Gatmon et al., 2001)" (p. 129). The relational model emphatically agrees, making it explicit that supervisors must take responsibility for initiating discussions of *all* difficult issues that arise, including issues of difference, because of the inhibiting impact upon supervisees of the power differential between supervisor and supervisee. (See chap. 1.)

Bernard and Goodyear (2014) emphasized that developing a strong supervisory relationship, based on shared goals, is a prerequisite for initiating difficult multicultural conversations. They referenced a study by Burkard et al. (2006) that made it clear supervisees who reported a useful discussion about a cultural issue were those who had *already* found their relationship with their supervisor to be productive and helpful. The relational model prioritizes creating a supervisory relationship in which difficult conversations can take place and intense affects can be processed.

Comfort with affect, another strong point of the relational supervisor, is an essential precondition for opening conversations around multicultural issues (Ladany et al., 2005). The relational model normalizes the emergence of intense affects. The relational supervisor's care in monitoring her supervisee's responses to her interventions, addressing ruptures when detected, and seeking consultation when tensions do not resolve creates a strong container for processing the disturbing emotional states that frequently accompany such conversations. In addition, the relational supervisor appreciates the potential clinical usefulness of working with disturbances in the supervisory relationship, cognizant that emotional work done in this way is likely to translate into new supervisee capacities in the clinical relationship. Processing "hot" material around difference in the supervisory relationship provides the supervisee with an experience that he can draw upon when his relationship with his patient becomes similarly emotionally "hot."

THE CONTRIBUTION OF RELATIONAL
PSYCHOANALYSIS TO WORKING WITH DIFFERENCE

Tummala-Narra (2015) critiqued classical psychoanalysis's failure to address sociocultural context and highlighted the contributions of relational psychoanalysis to the exploration of sociocultural issues in psychotherapy. She included among those contributions "recognition of historical trauma and neglect of sociocultural issues, indigenous cultural narratives, role of context in the use of language and expression of affect, influence of experiences of social oppression and stereotypes on therapeutic process and outcome, and the dynamic nature of cultural identifications" (p. 275). She called for psychoanalytic education and training curriculums to reflect the valuing of sociocultural issues and noted the challenge involved in training psychotherapists whose supervisors generally have less exposure to training in cultural competence than they do.

Michael Moskowitz, a psychoanalyst and organizer of the *Black Psychoanalysts Speak* conferences, in critiquing classical psychoanalytic culture, observed the following:

> Psychoanalysis suffers from a painful contradiction. At its core is a radical revisioning of culture and all forms of human relatedness. It asks us to examine those processes of self-deception that perpetuate both individual unhappiness and those social structures that benefit from inequality and oppression. Yet our psychoanalytic institutes have largely turned away from the big picture, the ills and inequalities of our cultures, and instead have focused on training and treating the relatively privileged. (Walt & Slome, 2015, p. 16)

Aron and Starr's (2013) revisioning of psychoanalysis emphasizes a form of psychotherapy and training that is meant *not* for the elite few but rather for *all* of the people. Their relational conception of psychoanalysis is based on the premise that clinicians need to open themselves to different ways of being in the world, including differences in culture and class. Aron and Starr invite contemporary practitioners to return to the values of early psychoanalytic practitioners who brought psychoanalytic practice to "the clinic" to address the suffering of those without the money to pay for treatment:

> The early analysts were not mainstream, high-income professionals; they were intellectuals, yes, but they were marginal, barely eked out a living . . . Marginality leaves one vulnerable. Being in touch with our vulnerability fuels our moral and ethical sensibility. (pp. 28–29)

Aron and Starr (2013) noted that the contemporary relational psychodynamic clinician—more likely to be female than male and more likely to be a lay mental health professional than a physician—finds herself in a position of relative marginality that echoes the situation of those pre–World War II European analysts. Contemporary relational clinicians are more vulnerable to discrimination from others (physicians, insurance companies) than were the male, medically dominated ego-psychological psychoanalysts of the 1950s and may therefore identify more readily with the marginalized, be more conscious of bias, be more available to consider their participation in destructive cultural patterns, and be less caught up in the dynamics of splitting, projection, and devaluation that were too common in classical psychoanalytic culture.

Aron and Starr's (2013) egalitarian rendition of psychoanalysis is premised upon Aron's (1996) relational view of authority, a view that my colleague and I built upon in constructing our model (Frawley-O'Dea & Sarnat, 2001). A supervisor who is willing to share authority with her supervisee, viewing the relationship as one of mutuality in the context of asymmetry, sets an example of openness and respecting difference in working with patients. She communicates to her supervisees: Take seriously the reality of difference, and get to know the other's point of view. Of course, despite the relational supervisor's willingness to negotiate what is "true," the relational psychoanalytic model is not simply relativistic. The model upholds a set of values that are broadly humane and psychological, such as the prizing of human connection; embracing interdependence as well as autonomy; and an appreciation for honesty, compassion, authenticity, and self-awareness. The model holds respect for cultural difference in dialectical tension with these foundational human values.

Much of the recent psychoanalytic work on difference derives from the relational school (Altman, 2006; Aron & Starr, 2013; Brickman, 2003; Cushman, 2000; Hamer, 2006; Hassinger, 2014; Layton, 2006; Leary, 2000; Tummala-Narra, 2004). Race, culture, and class are inherently social phenomena, and the relational approach studies such phenomena as they show up in a patient's inner life (Altman, 1995). In contrast, classical psychoanalytic models underestimated the importance of social phenomena, seeing them as mere "manifest content." Relational psychoanalytic authors have confronted the discomfiting reality that clinicians, however vigilant we might strive to be, operate, like all human beings, from what Layton (2006) called the *normative unconscious*: "the psychological consequences of living in a culture in which many norms serve the dominant ideological purpose of maintaining a power status quo" (pp. 238–239). Layton demonstrated how these cultural assumptions operated outside of her own awareness, shaping her attitudes toward and interventions with her patients. Even as she traced the troubling implications for that treatment, she offered no easy solutions.

HOW RELATIONAL PSYCHOANALYSTS WORK WITH DIFFERENCE

In this section, I present one brief and one extended vignette of relational psychoanalytic clinical work with racial difference. Racial difference stirs up profound conscious and unconscious responses within supervisors, supervisees, and patients. What we learn about navigating these treacherous waters stands us in good stead in working with other kinds of differences as well. Authors such as Hassinger (2014) and Suchet (2007) serve as virtual supervisors to us, showing through their self-analytic work how one facilitates the development of both supervisory and clinical competence in this arena.

Vignette 1

White, female, American psychoanalyst Hassinger (2014) showed how a clinician can, by attending to the flow of racially related enactments in an analysis, become aware of and begin to work with her unconscious participation in racist societal norms. She observed the emergence of her own unconscious attitudes toward both her patient's (African American) race and her own. Disturbing as this was for her, she embraced the experience as an opportunity to grow:

> In my dreams and waking reveries, errors and slips, [my patient] offered me the reclaiming of my confused, dissociated racialized self. When I told him I was writing about our work together, he was curious and pleased. Interestingly, he remarked, "I suppose you'll be exploring what race and racism have done to me." My answer: "I'm exploring what racism does to *us*." (pp. 339–340, emphasis added)

Hassinger's example of "self-supervision" through her self-analysis offers a model for supervisors.

A second vignette from the clinical literature illustrates, in more detail, relational psychoanalytic work with difference. Specifically, this psychoanalyst demonstrates the process of opening a conversation about race with a patient who defended against doing so; she also demonstrates how, through self-analysis, she began to access painful unconscious attitudes about her patient's race. Her interaction with her "internal supervisor" models how we may help our supervisees who struggle with similar issues.

Vignette 2

Part 1: Opening a Conversation About Race

Suchet (2007), a white woman raised in apartheid South Africa and practicing in New York, described her treatment of Justine, a professional black woman whose parents came from Guyana but who was raised in the West Indies. For a long time, Justine insisted that her choice of a white therapist meant nothing. Despite Suchet's efforts to raise the subject of race, the issue remained unspeakable for Justine. Suchet felt stymied as to how to open up what she knew must be an essential conversation. Suchet had felt that her failure to engage conversations about racial difference in other treatments had contributed to their ending prematurely.[2] This time, Suchet resolved to do better. As she put it, "If one believes in the inevitable structuring role of race in all our subjectivities, vigilance is necessary to make it visible" (p. 876).

Finally, Suchet asked Justine how she felt when she walked down the street in Manhattan. Justine disclosed, startlingly, "I used to think of my body as non-white, but now, I think, maybe I feel white" (p. 878). Suchet could then imagine that Justine's choice of a white psychotherapist might have expressed her unconscious wish to remain "unraced" or to even be "whitened." Justine's choice might also express compliance with the significant pressures from her mother to assimilate into the dominant race and culture.

Suchet observed that while Justine was trying, in fantasy, to feel part of the majority group in an effort to increase her sense of empowerment, engaging in this fantasy actually resulted in an enormous loss of personal power. She was replacing her black identity with an empty shell, leading to what Eng and Han (2000) dubbed "racial melancholia." As the treatment unfolded, Suchet and Justine found a link between Justine's melancholia and a previously denied early trauma: Justine had been sent as an infant to Guyana for a year to be cared for by an African nanny so that her mother might complete her graduate studies in the United States unencumbered. As this material emerged, Justine began to feel that her mother had sacrificed her for the "whiteness" of money and status. The therapeutic relationship deepened as this painful truth became real to Justine. Suchet observed, "Far from being unraced, race was central" (p. 880). She went on:

> . . . I know that nannies, mothers, black and white, power and loss are all interwoven [in this transference-countertransference]. [Justine's] psychodynamics are threaded through with racial meanings and overtones, as are mine. I know that this time I am . . . ready to embrace the racialized transferences that will inevitably oscillate between us. (p. 880)

---

[2]See Dalal (2006) on premature terminations as a consequence of inadequately engaging the topic of racial difference.

Discussion

A psychotherapist's ignorance, defensiveness, and/or anxiety about what would happen if the topic of race were to be engaged can lead to silencing of discussion about racial difference in racially diverse psychotherapy pairs. For a white psychotherapist, potential feelings of guilt about participating in racial privilege—as well as possible feelings of shame about failing to fulfill racialized ideals of whiteness (Altman, 2006)—make this conversation a dangerous one. For a nonwhite psychotherapist working with a white patient, the conversation may be even more dangerous. Psychotherapists of color live with the ever-present possibility of becoming receptacles for projected, unwanted parts of their white patient's selves, an everyday occurrence in our racist society, both in and out of the consulting room.

The same issues apply to racially diverse supervisory pairs. For a supervisor, even in a same-race supervisory dyad, it is easy to avoid talking about racial difference in the clinical dyad. The supervisor need only go along with the assumption that race is either "not the main issue here" or that now is not "a good time" to discuss it. A supervisor's conviction about the inevitable relevance of the subject and the importance of bringing it into the supervisory dialogue is essential. A supervisor must master her own anxieties well enough so that while she remains attuned to supervisee and patient anxiety—and exercises appropriate tact—she speaks to her supervisee and encourages her supervisee to speak to his patient. Relational psychoanalyst Leary (2000) pointed out that when issues of racial difference are spoken about in the psychotherapeutic situation and patient and psychotherapist become upset, the psychotherapist often feels that he has done something hurtful by broaching the subject. The supervisor must be ready to work with such feelings to untangle the transferences and countertransferences that can shut down therapeutic and supervisory dyads. A supervisor's prior invitations to her supervisee to speak about their own similarities and differences, whatever these may be, are helpful in preparing the supervisory space to hold such conversations.

Part 2: Working in the Countertransference (Developing Self-Awareness)

Suchet describes the work she did in the countertransference to integrate split-off racial memories from her own childhood. Suchet struggled to bear her feelings of culpability for her participation in South African culture as a white child who was cared for by a black nanny, enjoying the care and attention of the woman whose own children had to do without her. Suchet found it difficult to come to terms with how important her nanny was to her, how confusing her love for this nanny was, and how essential her nanny's blackness was to her embodied memory of intimacy with this beloved woman. Yet without embracing these memories, Suchet could not stay in emotional contact with her patient.

Suchet makes an analogy between working with racial material and working with impasse:

> By surrendering, the analyst accepts and acknowledges some failure of theirs that has contributed to the impasse.... The impasse has long historical roots in the withholding of recognition, in the inability to confer the other with the same subjectivity as the self. This impasse is tied to our refusal to accept our complicity in the destructiveness toward the other. Surrender [to the experience of the other] allows one to quell the internal fight over what "I am not" and what "I would never be" [that is, a racist]. In the acceptance of who one is, including all the not-me's, there is an opening up of the inner space.... This surrender implicates a process of remorse for the racist acts that have been and are perpetuated, directly and indirectly, individually and societally. (p. 883)

Discussion

The self-analytic work done by Suchet suggests how a relational supervisor might help a struggling supervisee grapple with the dynamics of racial difference. The relational psychodynamic supervisor, because she is prepared to take responsibility for her own contribution to difficulties, understands the need to find this experience of surrender and to help her supervisee to find it with her patient as well so that the supervisory and psychotherapeutic relationships may deepen.

The pathological defenses that racial difference evokes do damage to both the oppressed and the oppressor. It is not easy for either supervisor or psychotherapist to acknowledge that they hold unconscious feelings and fantasies about racial difference and enact them in ways that unwittingly contribute to tensions and blockages in the supervisory and psychother-apeutic relationships. Addressing difference demands taxing emotional work as supervisor and supervisee alike face frightening feelings, come to terms with their cultural identities, and acknowledge their participation in racism and other forms of prejudice, as oppressor or oppressed, how-ever unwitting and unwanted that participation may be.

We live in a racialized social world. We are primed from childhood to dissociate, diminish the significance of, or otherwise rationalize these features of our experience of self and other. We do it automatically, yet it requires ongoing unconscious psychic effort to keep these realities out of mind. This defensive effort debilitates both supervisor's and supervisee's capacity to function psychoanalytically. Allowing these disturbing realities to come to mind and talking about them when they do come to mind is an essential supervisory and psychotherapeutic competency. It is a com-petency that a relational model of psychodynamic supervision endorses and supports through its methods.

CONCLUSION

Suchet's work (2007) illustrates working with racial difference specifically, but the process she undergoes applies to work with any difference that evokes anxiety and leads to coping through splitting, projection, devalua-tion, and idealization. Marginalization and shame, as well as pathological defenses against shame, are ever-present threats for a person who is in a role that is perceived as "less than." Dominating, wounding, and then responding with feelings of guilt and defenses against guilt are ever-present possibilities for a person who is in a role that is perceived as "more than." I look forward to the day when relational supervisors, including myself, will be able to write as clearly and movingly about such experiences in supervision as Suchet has done in writing about treatment.

In the next chapter, we explore another issue that all supervisors work with: the ethical/legal dimension of supervision. Here, too, I believe that the relational model has something important to offer.

7

Common Supervisory Issues, Part III: Working With Legal and Ethical Issues

In this final chapter on common supervisory issues, I discuss the legal and ethical domain. Any psychologist opening such a discussion must begin by referencing the American Psychological Association's (APA) *Ethical Principles of Psychologists and Code of Conduct* (2010) and *Guidelines for Clinical Supervision in Health Service Psychology* (2014), and I refer the reader there for a more all-encompassing discussion of supervisor ethics. In this chapter, I limit myself to ethics topics that are particularly salient in working relationally in psychodynamic supervision. The chapter is divided into three parts, each of which approaches the intersection of legal and ethical issues and the relational model of psychodynamic supervision in a different way.

The first part highlights three issues that hold the potential for legal and ethical peril when working relationally: supervisee informed consent, appropriate maintenance of boundaries in supervision, and attending to the impact of supervisor disclosure. Given the experiential and personally

http://dx.doi.org/10.1037/14802-008
Supervision Essentials for Psychodynamic Psychotherapies, by J. E. Sarnat
Copyright © 2016 by the American Psychological Association.

intimate nature of the relational approach, supervisor clarity about these three issues helps to maintain a supervisory space of integrity.[1] The second part of this chapter emphasizes the affirmative contributions of the relational model to ethical supervisor conduct. In this section, I make the case that relational-model values provide scaffolding for ethical attitudes in supervision, and I use two vignettes to illustrate. In the third part, I offer some reflections on how the relational construction of power and authority, in particular, operates as an ethical force within psychodynamic supervision: first, by helping the supervisor to step back from the legacy of abuse of power in the psychoanalytic training tradition; and second, by sensitizing the supervisor to the destructive impact of subtly authoritarian teaching methods.

ETHICAL CHALLENGES FOR RELATIONAL SUPERVISORS

Supervisee Informed Consent

Standard 3.10 of APA's *Ethical Principles of Psychologists and Code of Conduct* (2010) states, in part, "When psychologists conduct ... consulting services ... they obtain the informed consent of the individual ..." (p. 6). Because the relational supervisor expects supervisees to make themselves personally vulnerable, it is essential that supervisees be provided the opportunity to give informed consent for this kind of supervisory experience. Supervisees need to know at the start of supervision that exploration of self is an essential part of the educational task of relational psychodynamic supervision and is intrinsic to working with countertransference. Therefore, a supervisee who chooses to engage in relational model psychodynamic supervision must consent to explore his psychology to the extent necessary to forward his training. Even if the supervisee is in his own treatment, which is highly recommended, the supervisor will expect the supervisee to be available to work on himself in supervision.

---

[1]See Thomas (2010, chapter 5) for a related discussion of the particular ethical challenges confronted by psychoanalytic supervisors (not specifically relational). She emphasized the areas of competence, multiple relationships, boundaries, and confidentiality.

The relational supervisor educates her supervisee about why she invites intimacy and openness in supervision. She explains the value of exploration of unconscious phenomena that arise in the supervisory relationship. She clarifies why it is necessary for a psychotherapist to understand his own psychology to do this challenging work and models openness to her own psychology. The supervisor also assures her supervisee that she will be thoughtful about what information she will reveal in her feedback to the training institution, although she carries responsibility to provide the training institution with what it needs to oversee the supervisee's education and progression. In these ways, the supervisor informs her supervisee about the process of relational supervision and also asks the supervisee to consent to a process that makes him vulnerable. In addition, the supervisor takes seriously her supervisee's fluctuating needs and anxieties in the course of the unfolding of the supervisory process, respecting how much vulnerability feels tolerable at any given moment. Consent is continually negotiated, rather than assumed to have been established in a single initial conversation or in signing an initial supervisory agreement. (See chap. 3 for more about this initial process of setting the frame and negotiating how to work together.) The supervisee should also be informed early on about procedures to be followed should difficulties arise. (See chap. 5 for a discussion of working with supervisees with difficulties.)

Appropriate Maintenance of Boundaries

Section 7.05(b) of the *Ethical Principles of Psychologists and Code of Conduct* (APA, 2010) is unequivocal about the need to separate teaching, with its evaluative component, and treating: "Faculty who are likely to be responsible for evaluating students' academic performance do not themselves provide that therapy" (p. 10). Because relational supervisory methods specifically include using clinical knowledge and technique in pursuit of an educational task—working with the supervisee's reactions to the patient, as well as to the supervisor—the question arises: Is this supervisory activity equivalent to treatment, and thus a violation of the teach–treat boundary?[2]

---

[2]See Thomas's (2010) assertion that "the teach–treat boundary . . . is another important ethical concept" (p. 61) in Frawley-O'Dea and Sarnat's (2001) model.

I believe that the supervisor does not breach the teach–treat boundary as long as the supervisor remains focused on the professional development of the supervisee (Sarnat, 1992; Whiston & Emerson, 1989). When the supervisor allows fidelity to the educational task to guide her choices about what material to explore and what to leave alone,[3] and the supervisee provides informed consent for working in this way, using clinical understanding to work with the supervisee's psychology—as it comes into play in his work with his patient and his work with his supervisor—violates no ethical principle. The supervisor also pays attention to how much and what kind of vulnerability is necessary to the educational task at hand; at times, she sets a limit when she feels the supervisee is going further into his personal issues than is necessary or helpful.[4]

Because the relational model's sanctioning of therapeutic technique to facilitate teaching may seem to some to create a "slippery slope" when it comes to other kinds of boundaries, it is especially important to articulate the model's view of the sexual/romantic boundary in supervision. I am in full accord with Standard 7.07 of the *Ethical Principles of Psychologists and Code of Conduct* (APA, 2010), which states, "Psychologists do not engage in sexual relationships with students or supervisees who are in their department, agency, or training center or over whom psychologists have or are likely to have evaluative authority" (p. 10). My colleague and I (Frawley-O'Dea & Sarnat, 2001) emphasize that any effort to rationalize a sexual relationship in relational-model supervision on the basis of the "mutuality" of the supervisory relationship would be inappropriate. An inherent relational and power violation exists in any sexual encounter between supervisor and supervisee, no matter how much the decision to do so might be "mutually negotiated."

Attending to the Impact of Supervisor Personal Disclosure

Because the relational supervisor brings in to supervision her personal reactions to the supervisee or the supervised case, special care must be

---

[3]See the vignette describing my work with Andrea, later in this chapter, for an example of material that I chose to leave alone.
[4]See the same vignette.

paid to the impact of such supervisor disclosures. It is important that supervisors have an understanding of good reasons—and not so good reasons—for making personal disclosures. I view this as a boundary issue. Although issues in disclosing personal reactions to a supervisee are not specifically addressed in the *Ethical Principles of Psychologists and Code of Conduct* (APA, 2010), Standard 3.08 clearly asserts that "Psychologists do not exploit persons over whom they have supervisory, evaluative, or other authority . . ." (p. 6), and in my view, supervisor disclosure may be exploitative if it is not made for the purpose of facilitating the supervisory process.

This volume includes a number of instances of my disclosing my experience to my supervisee. For example, in the transcript excerpted in chapter 4, I disclosed feeling touched by my supervisee, Jane, when she was able to confide to me the painful truth that she and her patient had "lost something" that they had between them earlier in their relationship. I did so in an effort to underline the importance of her acknowledgment and to bring the conversation into a more affective realm. In a vignette in chapter 1, I disclosed to a psychoanalytic candidate that I had sought consultation, as well as some of what I learned about my vulnerabilities through that consultation. In this case, I did so to release my supervisee from being the sole receptacle for the supervisory triad's feelings of shame and hopelessness. In a vignette in the second section in this chapter, I disclose to my supervisee that my feelings of guilt and anxiety had been "too hot to handle," which led me to split them off and project them into her. In this instance, I was bringing my supervisee's attention to a psychoanalytic concept that was part of our lived experience and attempting to free her from a toxic projective identification. In each of these cases, I made the judgment that the educational benefit of the disclosure outweighed the degree of potential disturbance to my supervisee. In each case, after disclosing, I paid attention to my supervisee's response and was prepared to work with that response.

The developmental stage of each supervisee is something I also keep in mind when considering whether to make a personal disclosure. Beginning supervisees often need to idealize their supervisors as a strategy for managing anxiety (Brightman, 1984–1985) and thus may find supervisor disclosure of anxiety or insecurity to be especially troubling. Whenever there is a power differential or a relationship of dependence, there also exists the possibility that disclosures made by the "parental" generation will feel overstimulating or even violating to the "younger generation." It is the ethical responsibility of the supervisor to consider such possible impact upon the supervisee. Some supervisees also need help to understand the difference between supervisor disclosure and psychotherapist disclosure, requiring clarification that the context for disclosure differs in the two relationships. A bond between senior and junior colleagues exists in supervision and differentiates the supervisory relationship from most therapeutic relationships. Talking about this difference can help the supervisee to think more clearly about the specific set of issues involved in deciding whether and what to disclose to a given patient.

Finally, although limited disclosure about the supervisor's life—family events, vacation destinations, and such—at times can contribute to the collegial bond, the supervisor needs to be mindful about whether such disclosures are being made in the service of the supervisory relationship or primarily to meet the needs of the supervisor. Similarly, discussion of shared professional interests can serve a mentoring function but if taken too far can exploit the supervisee as an admirer and become a distraction from the supervisory task. As always, supervisor self-awareness and self-discipline are essential in finding and implementing this balance.

HOW THE VALUES OF THE RELATIONAL MODEL SUPPORT ETHICAL SUPERVISOR CONDUCT

The relational model provides scaffolding for ethical attitudes and practices in supervision, as I hope to illustrate through two vignettes. The first is an account of supervisor ethical breaches, published by a supervisee, and the second is a vignette from my own experience as supervisor. Both vignettes show supervisors coping with concerns that a supervisee is failing to appropriately treat a patient. The supervisor's worry for the patient, feelings of culpability, and concerns about possible legal responsibility are all in play. In both, the supervisors become anxious, and when supervisors get anxious, they sometimes act out and lose their ethical compass.

Vignette 1: Nonrelational Supervisors React to "Inappropriate" Supervisee Behavior

Castellano (2013) described a traumatic experience that she underwent while being supervised at a psychodynamically oriented predoctoral externship. She was treating a patient, Anna, in a 20-session psychotherapy model. The process was rocky at the beginning, with Anna behaving in a passive-aggressive way and unable to open up and Castellano feeling angry and persecuted. In the fourth session, Castellano joined Anna sitting on the floor, having been asked by her patient to do so. As they sat together, Anna was able to open up. She disclosed a horrific story of physical, emotional, and sexual abuse at the hands of her older brothers and said that her parents did not notice or intervene.

Castellano described to each of her two supervisors what had happened, wanting their help but fearful of her supervisors' disapproval of her decision to join her patient on the floor. Each supervisor expressed concern. One told her to go ahead with sitting on the floor but to keep talking about it in supervision. The other, who was also the training director at the clinic, "vacillated between wanting me to 'meet Anna where she was at' and 'not wanting her to regress beyond what we can do for her'" in the limited sessions available (p. 725). Castellano, trying to make sense of these somewhat mixed messages, continued to sit on the floor with her patient for the next several sessions.

Castellano then presented her work with Anna at the agency case conference, which was led by the clinic director, Dr. A, whom Castellano hardly knew. In the presence of the group, Dr. A told Castellano that he was appalled that she was sitting on the floor with her patient and asked who had told her that such behavior was acceptable. When Castellano replied that her supervisors had, he replied that it was impossible that a licensed professional would have allowed her to think that decision was "appropriate." Dr. A later called Castellano into his office for what she described as a "tongue lashing." "I was unable to get a word in: First because Dr. A would just speak over me, and then later because I was rendered speechless through my tears" (p. 727). Dr. A asked nothing about Castellano's thinking about the case or about what was being discussed in her supervisions. He told Castellano that she had inappropriate boundaries and questionable clinical judgment, and that it had perhaps been a mistake to take her on as an extern.

When Castellano appealed to her supervisors for help with this traumatic experience, she received empathy from one, was told that the matter would "blow over" by both, and found that neither supervisor was willing to speak up for her to Dr. A. Both cited the hierarchical structure in the clinic. Castellano realized that she was in a situation similar to Anna's childhood situation: suffering abuse amidst a failure of the authorities to protect.

Castellano's supervisors were correct that the issue did "blow over." Incredibly, Dr. A never again mentioned his implied threat to terminate Castellano's externship nor anything else about his criticism of her and her work. Dr. A's silence left her doubting whether her memory of what had happened could be true.[5]

Despite her traumatization, Castellano felt that she was able to use one aspect of her experience constructively. She found that after the "tongue-lashing" she could empathize more fully than before with her patient's experience of abuse. She reported that her work with Anna deepened in the following session. Castellano tried to account for this shift, posing the question, "What happens when the therapist is a trainee and her supervisor reenacts the abuse experienced by the patient onto her?" (p. 720). She hypothesized that she "regressed in the service of Anna's ego" (p. 729). She and Anna were now victims together (rather than Castellano feeling persecuted by Anna), and the clinic director was now Castellano's persecutor.

---

[5]We may here recognize the power of dissociation in the face of trauma. Castellano stated that after leaving the internship, she repressed much of what had happened until, several years later, she participated in a list-serve discussion about boundary violations, which was moderated by a relational psychoanalyst. She was then finally able to think back over what had happened and decided to write about it.

Discussion

Castellano demonstrated her capacity to make lemonade out of lemons by utilizing her encounter with Dr. A to deepen her empathy with Anna's abject state and in her ability to think about the parallel processes involved. However, in her description of the impact of the director's attack on her, Castellano (as abusive survivors often do) seemed to partially justify Dr. A's abusive behavior, as if it were somehow inevitable that she would have to live out being persecuted by an authority as part of the parallel process. Here, I disagree. An abusive dynamic paralleling up from the patient *never* justifies acting out of abusive or nonprotective dynamics by supervisors.[6] Supervisors have an obligation to interrupt and analyze their participation in such parallel processes as soon as they become aware of them and to seek consultation if necessary. Instead, these supervisors appear to have remained blind to their participation in abusive and neglectful dynamics and continued to victimize the supervisee. According to Castellano's telling of the story, Dr. A shamed Castellano in the case conference in front of her peers, was verbally abusive to her in his office, did not self-reflect or apparently seek consultation, and failed to either follow through with her or, more appropriately, make a repair with her. In addition, Castellano's two individual supervisors were unwilling to confront their superior about his unethical treatment of their supervisee and left her to deal with the situation on her own. All of this adds up to seriously unethical supervisor behavior.[7]

Both of Castellano's discussants arrived at similar conclusions. Buechler (2013) commented that the character and defensive process of the supervisors (as portrayed) were equally as important as the parallel process: that personality shapes the limits of what can be projected into the supervisor. Goren (2013) cautioned, "As its very name implies, supervision involves inherent issues of power and authority that we need to remember make it rife for abuse" (p. 742).

---

[6]See Ladany and Bradley (2010) on the ethical imperative for supervisors to show respect for supervisees.

[7]According to the *Guidelines for Clinical Supervision in Health Service Psychology* (APA, 2014), "The 'professionalism covenant' puts the needs and welfare of the people [psychologists] serve at the forefront. . . . The essential components include: (1) integrity—honesty, personal responsibility and adherence to professional values; (2) deportment; (3) accountability; (4) concern for the welfare of others . . ." (p. 19).

In addition, Goren (2013) questioned whether Castellano, who was criticized by Dr. A for sitting on the floor with her patient, did anything "wrong" in the first place: The change of seat might be seen as an act of creativity rather than a violation. Goren also pointed out that the question of where Castellano sat, which aroused so much concern, was only one of many other transference-countertransference issues that her supervisors should have taken up with Castellano but did not. These commentaries illustrate the importance of introducing another (consultative) mind into a supervisory relationship in which powerful dynamics are in play.

Goren (2013) also commented on the silencing impact on the supervisee if a supervisor moralizes when a supervisor describes making nontraditional interventions. Mayer (1996) made a similar point, emphasizing that the judgmental attitudes of those to whom psychoanalytic psychotherapists present their work often lead them to hide what they actually do in their offices, and, as a consequence, "private conduct becomes more and more isolated from the potentially modulating influence of collegial scrutiny and public discussion" (p. 173). The intention of a supervisor who works from a relational model is to make it as safe as possible for a supervisee to bring what he actually *does* to supervision. She refrains from moralizing or shaming her supervisee, and if she fails in this, she will take responsibility for the impact of her reactivity upon her supervisee and work to repair it. The following example illustrates this approach.

Vignette 2: A Relational Supervisor Reacts to "Inappropriate" Supervisee Behavior

This vignette (Sarnat, 2006) captures a moment when I, like the supervisors in the previous vignette, became concerned that my supervisee was not doing right by her patient and, in response I became reactive. However, I handled the situation differently. I am aware that mine was an intrinsically less challenging situation than that faced by Castellano's supervisors because abuse dynamics were not reverberating up and down the supervisory triad, and I am not suggesting that I am above making ethical errors, especially when under duress. None of us are. I juxtapose these two vignettes to illustrate how my model of supervision contributed, at least in part, to my recovering from and repairing the initial error.

Andrea let me know in our first supervisory hour that the patient whom she wanted to present to me, Doug, had cancelled his last three sessions. She told me that she had "avoided" talking about this case with her previous supervisor. Nor was Andrea talking with Doug about the cancellations. She explained that because he regularly called and told her why he was cancelling, she felt no need to "make an issue of it."

I found her account troubling. What was going on that such things were not being talked about? And why did Andrea seem so apparently unconcerned about Doug's withdrawal? Was she not worried that he might drop out of treatment? Although I was distressed by her account, I did not take it up in this hour because it felt too soon to plunge into such sensitive territory. I limited myself to trying to put into words what I thought Andrea could be picking up about Doug that might have led her to act in this way, hoping that articulating this might allow her to reflect on her avoidance and work with it.

This was not the case. In the next supervisory hour, Andrea announced that Doug had canceled his fourth session in a row and, in telling me, she again treated the cancellation as a kind of nonissue. I became anxious that I was failing to meet my responsibility to the patient to receive competent treatment. (See *Guidelines for Clinical Supervision in Health Service Psychology* [APA, 2014], Domain G, Section 2, "Supervisors uphold their primary ethical and legal obligation to protect the welfare of the client/patient" [p. 25].) I said, with an edge in my voice, "It's hard for me to understand why you don't feel more concerned about why Doug isn't showing up. This is a real problem in the therapy and you seem almost not to care!" Andrea looked shocked. Noting that, I became aware of my reactivity, and tried to "walk it back," suggesting that we think together about why she might be responding in the way that she was. As she spoke to me, it became clear that the issue was *not* that Andrea did not care. Becoming reflective, she was able to say, "Actually, what's happening with Doug makes me think about the trouble I have standing up for myself in certain intimate relationships. If that's what's going on here, maybe it means that I withdrew because confronting Doug makes me uncomfortable."

I was relieved, of course, that Andrea was beginning to think about her motives, rather than continuing to rationalize the problem, and my concerns about her diminished. When Andrea started to tell me the details of her difficulties standing up for herself in intimate relationships, I stopped her, feeling that this kind of detail was not necessary to our supervisory task and that my permitting her to continue might create confusion about my supervisory (as opposed to therapeutic) role. In any case, I felt that we hadn't established enough trust to warrant Andrea's making herself so vulnerable to me, and managing intimacy/distance seemed like a countertransference issue with which Andrea might need my help.

In the next supervisory hour, Andrea began by reporting that she had called Doug and told him that she thought that more than just "work pressures" were causing him to miss his appointments and that he needed to come in so they could talk about it. Doug showed up for his next hour! I was impressed with the use that Andrea had made of our session, and told her so.

In defining the supervisory frame in our first session, I had explicitly requested that Andrea tell me if anything in our supervision made her feel uncomfortable. Now Andrea took me up on my invitation, going back to the previous supervisory hour. She said that she had felt upset to see how her own anxieties had interfered with her work with Doug and realized it had undermined her confidence in herself as a therapist. She said that she knew I had been right to bring it up but that the session had nonetheless left her feeling overwhelmed and exposed. I replied that I could understand her feeling that way, that I appreciated her ability to reflect on these issues, and that all therapists need to work on such things, including myself. Andrea then fell silent. Aware that her comments had been self-critical but had shielded me from criticism, I asked her if she had anything more to say about our interaction last time. She said she didn't, and assured me that it was resolved now. But then she said, as if in passing, that if I had asked her right after our last meeting, *then* she might have had some feedback for me. I, of course, inquired about what she might have said at the time. Her answer: "I guess that it got a little too intense. And I didn't understand why you suddenly had such a strong reaction when the previous week you didn't take issue at all with what I was doing with

Doug." I acknowledged that my response to her work with Doug had suddenly shifted and that I could imagine that this might have been shocking for her. I also noted the accuracy of her observation about my tone. I said that I thought that my feelings of worry for the patient and my feelings of being a neglectful supervisor had made me anxious, which had led me to speak to her in an accusatory way:

> I think that my feelings were too hot for me to handle at that moment, and so I passed the "hot potato" to you. We could think of it as a failure of containment on my part, and a projective identification into you of what I couldn't bear.

Andrea was intrigued by my observation that she had been the recipient of a projective identification, something that she had never been able to identify before and that had previously been a pure abstraction in her mind. I imagine that she also felt relieved because I was, in effect, releasing her from that projective identification by taking responsibility for it.

Andrea finally, then, presented a session with Doug. He had told Andrea that the anniversary of his wife's death had just passed and that he had been feeling the need to be alone during these past weeks, avoiding his friends. Andrea told him that she felt touched by his willingness to confide this to her and then added, "Maybe that's why you needed to stay away from our sessions, too."

Andrea described this interaction with some tentativeness, concerned because she had not made a "fuller" transference interpretation. I told her that I thought her response was just right—both accurate and tactful—and that anything more might have detracted from the naturalness of the interchange. I added that helping Doug to become aware of his tendency to withdraw from her at moments of vulnerability, exploring his reasons for doing so, and then helping him to reconnect might be one goal for Doug's therapy. Andrea responded that this formulation gave her a sense, for the first time, of what she and Doug were trying to do.

As we discussed this, I was thinking about parallel issues in our supervisory relationship, noting the incidents of withdrawal from connection on each of our parts at moments of vulnerability in these opening supervisory hours. I did not talk about this, feeling that we had done quite enough for one session and that her good work with Doug needed to stay front and center. There was no educational reason for me to disclose my thoughts at that point, especially since modulating intimacy was something with which Andrea likely needed my help. On the other hand, when and if Andrea seemed to be disconnecting from Doug or me, or the intensity of intimacy in either relationship seemed to be becoming too much, I might bring us back to it. My goal would be to use my understanding to strengthen our supervisory relationship, as well as to help Andrea to understand herself and deepen her work with Doug and other patients.

Discussion

This second example illustrates several ways in which relational-model values contribute to ethical supervisor conduct. We see a supervisor monitoring herself and trying to self-correct at a moment of reactivity. Later, the supervisor acknowledges the mutuality of the supervisory relationship by referring to the limits of her own capacity to manage her anxiety. The vignette also shows a supervisor taking responsibility for the asymmetry of the power relationship by directly inviting negative feedback, rather than expecting the supervisee to volunteer it. In addition, the supervisor demonstrates mindfulness about appropriate boundaries for supervisee disclosure by declining when the supervisee volunteers to self-disclose details of her personal relationship patterns when the disclosure does not seem likely to enhance either immediate learning or the supervisory relationship. We also see appropriate supervisor disclosure, when the supervisor acknowledges her own anxiety and defense to free her supervisee from a burdensome state of mind. In these ways, relational concepts led me to a more ethical supervisory stance than Castellano's (2013) supervisors apparently were able to take.

As a supervisee experiences his supervisor taking responsibility for errors and working to repair them in the supervisory relationship, he develops an ethical compass of his own. When a supervisor demonstrates acceptance of the inevitability of her own mistakes, she models[8] for the

---

[8]See *Guidelines for Clinical Supervision in Health Service Psychology* (APA, 2014), Domain G, Section 1: "Supervisors model ethical practice ..." (p. 24).

supervisee nondefensiveness and curiosity about what is happening in the moment in a relationship. The supervisee thus develops an analytic attitude toward the enactments that he inevitably participates in with his patients. When a supervisor makes the medium the message—talking openly with her supervisee about difficult things as she urges the supervisee to talk openly with his patient about difficult things—she models integrity for the supervisee.

THE RELATIONAL CONSTRUCTION OF AUTHORITY AS AN ETHICAL FORCE

The relational construction of authority contributes to ethical supervisory attitudes and conduct. In this section, we take a closer look at how this view of authority makes a difference.

Interrupting Supervisor Abuses of Power

Castellano's (2013) paper, of course, is not the only account of abusive supervisor treatment in the literature. A transgenerational transmission of abusive authority relations has gone unchecked within psychoanalytic supervision for too many years. Sadly, the psychoanalytic legacy of abuse of power in training dates to Freud's way of relating to his "disciples." (See Introduction.) In the final chapter of *The Supervisory Relationship* (Frawley-O'Dea & Sarnat, 2001), we presented an extended vignette illustrating abuse of power in a psychoanalytic institute, and several examples of abuses in training psychodynamic psychotherapists are described in *Power Games* (Raubolt, 2006). I contributed a chapter to that book on the relational view of authority to elaborate a framework for healthier power relations in psychoanalytic training (Sarnat, 2006). I draw upon that chapter here.

Enhancing Nonauthoritarian Teaching

The relational model of psychodynamic supervision, beyond interrupting frank abuses of authority, also offers an alternative to teaching styles that are subtly authoritarian. The transformative power of the supervisory relationship is understood to reside in the creation of an atmosphere of mutual vulnerability, with the supervisor encouraging the empowerment of her supervisee, rather than using her own power to impress or intimidate. The quality of the relationship is the source of the supervisor's authorization to exercise influence, as the supervisor holds lightly her role as didactic teacher and is prepared to let it go to respond to an emerging supervisory process. "Here surprise and discovery are as much a part of the supervisor's experience as they are a part of the supervisee's experience. Both participants are learners as well as teachers" (Sarnat, 2006, p. 258).

A relational supervisor does not exploit the culturally ingrained compliance of her supervisees. As Cooper and Gustafson (1985) put it, "In order to be loyal to traditional authority and give them [e.g., supervisors] the power and deference one assumes unconsciously they deserve and need, [the supervisee] willingly sacrifices . . . the capacity to think clearly, critically and independently" (p. 8). In a relational model of supervision, a nondeferential teaching and learning relationship is the goal, even if that entails moments of tension and conflict between supervisee and supervisor.

CONCLUSION

In this chapter, I have, first, highlighted ethical areas that require special attention from the relational supervisor because of the intimacy and intensity of the relational way of working. Second, I have tried to show how enculturation in a relational approach supports ethical supervisor behavior in stressful situations. Third, I have emphasized how the relational model's view of authority, in particular, functions as an ethical force, modifying a psychoanalytic tradition rife with abuses of power as well as subtly authoritarian attitudes toward teaching.

In the next chapter, in considering future directions for a relational model of supervision, I include among my "wish list" the routine provision of consultation to supervisors. A supervisor needs both a model of supervision that promotes ethical practice and the consultative input of emotionally available colleagues to sustain it.

8

Future Directions

In this final chapter, I imagine a future of increased psychodynamic supervisory effectiveness. In this future, supervisors will take to heart the findings of research and choose to augment traditional methods with relational and experiential techniques and also make use of technology. I envision an expansion of supervisor training and the provision of ongoing consultation to supervisors, as well as support for more research that links supervision process variables to supervisee learning outcomes. I begin, though, by exploring some of the impediments to making such changes. Throughout this chapter, I draw on previous work (Sarnat, 2012).

http://dx.doi.org/10.1037/14802-009
Supervision Essentials for Psychodynamic Psychotherapies, by J. E. Sarnat
Copyright © 2016 by the American Psychological Association.

RESISTANCES TO EMBRACING THE RELATIONAL MODEL OF PSYCHODYNAMIC SUPERVISION

The research literature from cognitive psychology, education, and psychodynamic psychotherapy, cited in chapter 2, has made an implicit interpretation to psychodynamic supervisors: Didactic teaching and simple skill development in supervision will not suffice. We must engage experientially with supervisees and reflect upon our supervisory relationships if we are to become more effective in teaching the art of psychodynamic psychotherapy. Addressing resistances to that "interpretation"—one of the goals of all of my writing on supervision—is necessary if we are to improve supervisory methods.

It is not difficult to imagine why some psychodynamic supervisors might continue to rely upon nonrelational, patient-centered, didactic approaches rather than embracing relational methods. For some, the choice to do so might reflect a commitment to a clinical theory that is nonrelational. However, even some clinicians who identify with relational clinical ideas may not appreciate the need for their supervisory theory to match their clinical theory, or they may be reluctant to bring this approach into supervision for fear of breaching the teach–treat boundary. (See chap. 7 for discussion of relational psychodynamic supervision and the teach–treat boundary.) Still other supervisors may unthinkingly continue to perpetuate the tradition in which they themselves had been supervised. Finally, some may be reluctant to give up the prerogative of being the "objective expert" in their supervisory role, an understandably hard-to-relinquish position given the emotional chaos that often engulfs us when we function as clinicians.

Working relationally presents obvious challenges. Talking with one's supervisee about the supervisory relationship can evoke intense affects. These can make a supervisor uncomfortable, especially if she is not sufficiently clear about why doing so is necessary to facilitate supervisee development. In addition, supervisors are naturally reluctant to see ways in which their own participation in the supervisory relationship has a negative impact on their supervisees and, sometimes, on the patient.

We all resist such painful truths. Yet I invite readers who may have resisted taking on such challenges or for whom a relational way of working may be a departure from how they were trained to consider experimenting with this approach. In my view, doing so means moving into the future.

EMBRACING TECHNOLOGIES:
AUDIO AND VIDEO RECORDING

Although it is considered standard practice by most nonpsychodynamic supervisors, video and audio recording of clinical hours is still all too rare among the psychodynamic supervisors with whom I am acquainted. Some of this lag in the use of technology may be a result of supervising in private offices rather than having access to a fitted-out training clinic. Current technological improvements promise to do away with such technical obstacles.

Yet beyond the practical challenges of using technology, I have observed active distrust of recording among many psychodynamic supervisors. Some view recordings as breaking into the "sanctity" of the psychotherapy hour, destroying the patient's—and the psychotherapist's—privacy, and thus disturbing the psychoanalytic situation. Such wholesale rejection of recording is based on outdated ideas about what facilitates and hampers the development of trust in a clinical relationship. In my experience, being observed means different things in different relationships, and those meanings change over time. Supervisor reluctance to tape may also reflect ignorance of the educational benefit for a supervisee of having his actual work observed. All supervisees have blind spots that prevent them from verbally reporting to their supervisors some of the countertransference and technical issues with which they need help. Supervisors also need to make use of all possible means to access nonsemantic aspects of the patient and the therapeutic relationship (Schore, 2011), phenomena that are less likely to find their way into a process note or supervisee verbal report.

Kernberg (2010) challenges the assumption made by many psychoanalysts that recordings inevitably disrupt the psychotherapeutic process. Watkins (2013) offers empirical evidence for Kernberg's assertion: "(1) when informed consent is given, we have no actual evidence of such harm caused by session recording, and (2) it indeed appears that valid psychoanalytic work can be carried out under recording conditions (Bucci & Maskit, 2007; Siegel et al., 2002)" (p. 9). My personal experience has borne this out. Most patients are able to tolerate being recorded, especially when the supervisor is available to explore the feelings that are evoked in supervisee and patient by the process and to think through with the supervisee the impact that introducing taping is having on the therapeutic and supervisory relationships. For those (unusual) patients who are uncomfortable about being observed by a supervisor, exceptions should be made. But, in my view, the benefits outweigh the costs for most clinical dyads.

Some supervisors are uncomfortable, as well, fearing that recordings take away supervisees' freedom to unconsciously organize what they bring to the supervisory hour. Citing the psychoanalytic clinical dictum that "the patient determines the content of the hour," these supervisors want their supervisees to have the same privilege. This concern, although an expression of the value placed by psychoanalytic practitioners on privacy and containment, may also reflect some confusion about the difference between supervisory methods and clinical methods: Free association is not the primary method by which supervisees communicate with their supervisors. I have found that if I allow the supervisee to decide which portion of the recording to focus on initially—and I pay attention to the anxieties and conflicts that come up for the supervisee in discussing the recording—trust will develop and I can, over time, intervene more freely, as needed. Supervisors have the right—and the obligation[1]—to ask their supervisees to bear the anxieties of confronting their "growing edges"—even when seeing and hearing them on a screen or coming from a speaker is painful—although we must, of course, help our supervisees to bear that pain and make strenuous efforts to mitigate their feelings of shame.

---

[1]According to the Guidelines for Clinical Supervision in Health Service Psychology: "2. Supervisors uphold their primary ethical and legal obligation to protect the welfare of the client/patient. 3. Supervisors serve as gatekeepers to the profession. Gatekeeping entails assessing supervisees' suitability to enter and remain in the field" (American Psychological Association, 2014, p. 26).

Presentation of process notes and playing of recordings are modalities that each make sense for teaching certain supervisees in certain situations. Making use of the full range of options, including recording technologies, will enhance the field of psychodynamic supervision.

NEW POSSIBILITIES

I can imagine a number of new possibilities for psychodynamic supervision as it continues to evolve in its second century. These include supplementing the training of psychotherapists with outside-of-supervision experiential exercises; increasing the availability of supervisor training; building in more consultation for supervisors; and whenever possible, bringing organization-based supervisors together in teams.

Experiential Learning Outside of Supervision

Learn-by-Doing Practice Models for Novice Psychotherapists

Traditional supervisory methods of teaching novice therapists—methods that require that the supervisee be thrown in with patients before they can receive the help of a supervisor—are educationally and possibly even ethically questionable. Not only our supervisees, but also their patients will benefit if we provide supervisees with laboratory experiences for skill development before putting supervisees face-to-face with human beings who are in immediate psychological pain. Safran and Muran (2000) and Cabaniss, Cherry, Douglas, and Schwartz (2011) have created focused, participatory teaching exercises that are available to help beginners start to develop complex clinical skills.

As we move into the future, I hope that psychodynamic training settings will follow Binder's (2011) recommendation to add "learn-by-doing" practice models that employ interactive computer programs and videos. Using these materials, a beginning therapist responds to a progressively graded series of situations, such as working with an angry or demeaning client, before having to confront such a client in the flesh. These pedagogical strategies have been adopted by few psychodynamic training settings, at least among those with which I am familiar. For such "analog" training to become more broadly available, departments of psychology, in collaboration with computer science departments, could disseminate their interactive technological innovations for use outside of academia.

Self-Awareness Training for Expert Psychotherapists

However, beginning clinicians are not the only ones who can benefit from structured, participatory teaching exercises to hone the art of conducting psychoanalytic treatment. Recently, at the meetings of the International Psychoanalytic Association, preconference workshops have been offered, including "Listening-to-Listening," developed by Haydee Faimberg. Analysts convene in small groups to review transcripts of analytic sessions, divided into units of 5 minutes of clinical process and distributed sequentially. Participants thus have the opportunity to experience the unfolding of the clinical hour almost as the analyst did. During discussion of the transcripts, a group of three analyst-facilitators listens for and reflects back to the participants their sense of how each analyst-member's inferences about the session reflect his particular theoretical assumptions. These workshops create a setting in which the reality that theories are lenses is highlighted, and growth in psychoanalyst self-awareness is stimulated.

Mindfulness Training

Neuroscience-based techniques offer another opportunity to broaden and deepen the educational experience of our supervisees. To help supervisees develop their capacity for reverie and to tolerate the disturbing feelings stirred by their patients and the treatment process, psychotherapy training programs might, as Safran and Muran (2000) have already done, supplement psychotherapy supervision with training in meditation. Ulmer's (2011) approach to utilizing mindfulness techniques to enhance the calm, emotional availability of supervisors who are interacting with distraught supervisees is equally intriguing.

The Importance of Supervisor Education

The field of supervisor education is a work in progress. I have personally witnessed significant development in this area during the past 40 years. In my own doctoral and postdoctoral training (I received my PhD in 1975), I received no training in supervision, and on the day I received my psychology license, the director of my clinic assigned me two interns to supervise. This was not uncommon. Since that time, courses on supervision have become common in some parts of the country. In the San Francisco Bay Area, supervision training is alive and well. Supervision classes are required at all of the local PsyD programs and some internship sites, and numerous continuing education courses for licensed mental health practitioners are offered annually. At my institute, The Psychoanalytic Institute of Northern California, a year-long supervision seminar, followed by a year of mentoring, is required of all analysts who supervise candidates. An exemplary postlicensure supervision training program has been in operation for more than two decades at The Psychotherapy Institute in Berkeley. Yet in many parts of the country, much work in implementing training for supervisors remains to be done (Watkins, 2013).

The value of supervisor education is obvious. Focused study allows new supervisors to become aware of a variety of supervisory approaches and of the evidence for effective supervisory practice. In my experience, supervisors who have had an opportunity to reflect on the process of supervision become more engaged in the art and are at less risk for mindlessly perpetuating the limitations of their own supervisors.

Observing other supervisors in action is a vital aspect of supervisor education and one that deserves further development. The APA Psychotherapy Supervision Video Series (http://www.apa.org/pubs/videos) is, therefore, a welcome contribution to supervisor education.

Training supervisors to use learning objectives could improve the effectiveness of psychodynamic supervision. Moga and Cabaniss (2014) made a convincing case for the pedagogical importance of clearly defined and assessable learning objectives for the supervision of psychodynamic psychotherapy and psychoanalysis: "Several studies (Cabaniss et al., 2003;

Kernberg, 1986; Pegeron, 1996; Rojas et al., 2010) have indicated that without clear objectives, supervisees are unclear about the goals of the process and anxious about evaluation" (p. 529). Moga and Cabaniss, based on an extensive literature review, defined the five universally endorsed learning areas for teaching psychoanalytic treatment: analytic listening, creating and deepening analytic process, using interventions that allow for the elaboration of unconscious material and deepen the transference, the capacity for formulation based on a theory about change, and the capacity for self-analysis. They therefore recommended that each "learning community" design measurable learning objectives based on these five areas, individualizing the objectives to the specific values and goals of the particular training organization. This proposal offers a pathway toward enriching supervisor training, making it more intentional and effective, while refraining from imposing rigid schemas from outside. The proposal is a lovely way of bringing together the benefits of a "hard-headed" approach with the "unique and peculiar" qualities of psychoanalytic relationships at their best. (See the Introduction for a discussion of how this polarity plays out within psychoanalysis.)

Building in Supervisory Consultation

In my view, just as no ethical clinician would forgo consultation, neither should an ethical supervisor do so. Yet supervisory consultation is the exception in the field at large, rather than the rule. We need to change the culture of supervisors to make seeking consultation ordinary. Many supervisors carry an idea—part of the old psychoanalytic legacy perhaps—that if their level of seniority makes them competent to supervise, they should need no consultative help. Nothing could be further from the truth. The more one realizes how much is going on unconsciously in the supervisory relationship, the more one appreciates the ongoing need for a third mind, no matter how "senior" one might be.

"Burnout" and vicarious traumatization affect supervisors just as they affect psychotherapists. When supervisors listen to disturbing material, it is important for them to have a place to bring their emotional responses to the work. Consultation is also necessary to protect the supervisee from being the person to whom the supervisor turns for care. In my experience, supervisors do at times "steal" care from their supervisees, looking at their supervision hours as needed breaks in a grueling clinical day and slipping into a collegial or informal mentoring role at the expense of the training needs of the supervisee. Supervisors need to feel that they have the right—and even the obligation—to seek out the dedicated attention of peers, paid consultants, and personal psychotherapists. The learning that happens in consultation keeps the work fresh and meaningful. When I encounter a new way to think about something that I am caught in with a supervisee— whether it be offered by an author, a colleague, a paid consultant, my own psychoanalyst, or even through my own writing process—I grow, as does my supervisee.

Team Approaches to Supervising

When I consult to licensed psychotherapists in my private practice, I work as an individual practitioner. But when I supervise within psychotherapy and psychoanalytic training programs, I have the opportunity to work in a team, collaborating with others who supervise the same student. Teams, too, can be places to think and grow.

It can be helpful for a supervisor to discuss the supervisee's progress with other supervisors who inevitably experience the supervisee some- what differently. Talking together about the supervisee may not only help each supervisor to understand the supervisee in fuller dimension, but also clarify something about each supervisor's way of relating to the supervisee (Ebbert, 2011). In my experience, supervisees feel "seen" and cared about when their supervisors collaborate on behalf of their training.

Team meetings also provide an opportunity to work with splitting dynamics that can parallel up from a case into the supervisory team and complicate the relationship not only between clinicians, but also between supervisors (Dent, 2007). Formulating splitting dynamics in a team con- versation and helping the supervisee to see that different aspects of his patient—and himself—are showing up in different supervisory relation- ships provides a powerful opportunity for experiential learning.

EXPANDING RESEARCH

Finally, I hope that our field can continue to generate research relating process and outcome in psychodynamic supervision. Falender and Shafranske (2004) and Watkins (2011, 2013, 2015) commented upon the limitations of current research in supervision. Falender and Shafranske observed that many studies surveyed supervisees about what they *liked* in a supervisor, but few collected independent data about the actual *effectiveness* of various approaches to supervising.

Watkins (2010) observed that the research literature on the supervisory alliance is still "very much in its infancy" (p. 393). I am eager for research that shows how the quality of the supervisory relationship affects supervisee learning. Bernard and Goodyear (2014) observed that two specific areas of supervision research are currently in favor, one of which they called "particular relationship processes, e.g., working alliance; attachment" (p. 299). This focus of current research interest suggests that we may soon know more about the predictive value of "good" supervisory relationships.

Psychoanalytic research on supervision process is taking place in Scandinavia. Szecsödy (1990, 2008, 2012, 2013) has studied the impact of supervisor mutuality and process focus in supervision, an interesting line of inquiry because of its potential to validate (or invalidate) the effectiveness of the relational model. He has called for more descriptive, empirical research—based on audio or video recordings and transcripts of those recordings—following supervisory dyads over time. Such studies would show what supervisors actually do, not what they say they do.

In addition, Szecsödy's (2008) adaptation of Tuckett's (2005) "psychoanalytic frames" as a training and research tool for supervision deserves to be more widely adopted. Use of these "supervisory frames"—the participant-observational frame, the supervisory conceptual frame, the supervisory interventional frame, and the evaluation frame—could provide conceptual direction and coherence in studying psychodynamic supervision process and linking it to learning outcomes.

CONCLUSION

And so this monograph comes to an end. It has been my intention to enlarge my readers' sense of what is possible in supervision and to embolden them to try something new. I also hope that my readers come away with a felt sense of what it is like to be engaged in a relational psychodynamic supervision, as well as having some understanding of the evidence that suggests the effectiveness of this approach. I would be most gratified if the reader were stimulated by this volume to further explore the growing literature on relational psychodynamic supervision. (See appendix). I hope that I have encouraged my supervisor-readers to invest in the quality of the supervisory relationships that they create with their students. I hope that I have empowered my supervisee-readers to advocate with their supervisors for the kind of relationship that works best for them. My work will have served its purpose if it enables some supervisory pairs to find their way to an enriched and enlivened supervisory relationship.

Appendix:
An Annotated List of
Readings on Relational
Psychodynamic Supervision

Beck, J., Sarnat, J., & Barenstein, V. (2008). Psychotherapy-based approaches to supervision. In C. A. Falender & E. P. Shafranske (Eds.), *Casebook for clinical supervision: A competency-based approach* (pp. 57–96). Washington, DC: American Psychological Association. http://dx.doi.org/10.1037/11792-004

   Case material presented by three supervisors of different theoretical orientations, all of whom are process-consistent in their supervisory approach, and one of whom (Sarnat) uses a relational psychodynamic approach.

Bergmann, M. S. (2003). A contribution to the supervisory panel. *Psychoanalytic Dialogues, 13,* 327–339. http://dx.doi.org/10.1080/10481881309348737

Frawley-O'Dea, M. G. (2003). Supervision is a relationship too: A contemporary approach to psychoanalytic supervision. Symposium on psychoanalytic training and education. *Psychoanalytic Dialogues, 13,* 355–366. http://dx.doi.org/10.1080/10481881309348739

Black, M. J. (2003). Afterword. *Psychoanalytic Dialogues, 13,* 367–375.

   A panel including the commentaries of two supervisors—one classical psychoanalytic (Bergmann), the other relational psychoanalytic (Frawley-O'Dea)—on the same two case reports. Black compares and contrasts these supervisory approaches.

Berman, E. (2000). Psychoanalytic supervision: The intersubjective development. *International Journal of Psychoanalysis, 81,* 273–290.

   A complex and textured presentation of the intersubjective perspective on supervision.

Brown, L., & Miller, M. (2002). The triadic intersubjective matrix in supervision. *International Journal of Psychoanalysis, 83,* 811–823.

Demonstrates how a supervisor's willingness to work with his own unconscious material initiated an associative process that led to a deepening of the analytic work.

Burka, J., Sarnat, J., & St. John, C. (2007). Learning from experience in case conference: A Bionian approach to teaching and consulting. *International Journal of Psychoanalysis, 88,* 981–1000. http://dx.doi.org/10.1516/W766-4007-8205-5478

How consultation, using Bionian and intersubjective principles, helped a case conference leader release her case conference from a stuck place and become an effective working group.

Caligor, L., Bromberg, P., & Meltzer, J. (Eds.). (1984). *Clinical perspectives on the supervision of psychoanalysis and psychotherapy.* New York, NY: Plenum Press.

An edited collection of papers on supervision, written from an interpersonal psychoanalytic perspective, upon which Frawley-O'Dea and Sarnat (2001) drew in developing their relational model.

Frawley-O'Dea, M. G., & Sarnat, J. (2001). *The supervisory relationship: A contemporary psychodynamic approach.* New York, NY: Guilford Press.

A relational model of supervision intended for training therapists to work in contemporary clinical registers.

McKinney, M. (2000). Relational perspectives and the supervisory triad. *Psychoanalytic Psychology, 17,* 565–584.

This article expands the definition of parallel process to include a system of multidirectional influence.

Ogden, T. H. (2005). On psychoanalytic supervision. *International Journal of Psychoanalysis, 86,* 1265–1280. http://dx.doi.org/10.1516/BEE8-C9E7-J7Q7-24BF

How the supervisor helps the psychotherapist to enter into reverie and "dream the patient."

Pegeron, J. P. (1996). Supervision as an analytic experience. *Psychoanalytic Quarterly, 65,* 693–710.

An argument for—and illustration of—how the process of supervision can itself be analytic.

Rock, M. H. (Ed.). (1997). *Psychodynamic supervision: Perspectives of the supervisor and the supervisee.* Northvale, NJ: Jason Aronson.

An edited collection of papers on psychodynamic supervision, many of which are written from a relational perspective.

Sarnat, J. (1992). Supervision in relationship: Resolving the teach/treat dilemma in psychoanalytic supervision. *Psychoanalytic Psychology*, *9*, 387–403.

How the interpersonal shift created by an intersubjective view of the supervisory relationship creates a context in which the "teach versus treat" dilemma may be less problematic.

Sarnat, J. (1997). The contribution of a process-oriented case conference to the development of students in the first year of a doctor of psychology program. *The Clinical Supervisor*, *15*(2), 163–180. http://dx.doi.org/10.1300/J001v15n02_12

A description of developmental processes in beginning doctoral students and how to work with them relationally in case conference.

Sarnat, J. (1998). Rethinking the role of regressive experience in psychoanalytic supervision. *Journal of the American Academy of Psychoanalysis*, *26*, 529–543.

An argument for normalizing regressive experiences in supervision.

Sarnat, J. (2006). Authority relations in psychodynamic supervision: A contemporary view. In R. Raubolt (Ed.), *Power games: Influence, persuasion, and indoctrination in psychotherapy training* (pp. 255–271). New York, NY: Other Press.

A further elaboration of the view of authority relations in supervision that was sketched out in *The Supervisory Relationship* (Frawley-O'Dea & Sarnat, 2001).

Sarnat, J. (2008). Reuniting the psychic couple in analytic training and practice: A candidate's experience. *Psychoanalytic Psychology*, *25*, 110–121. http://dx.doi.org/10.1037/0736-9735.25.1.110

A reflection on the importance of unconscious processes in psychoanalytic training based on my own experience as a candidate.

Sarnat, J. (2010). Key competencies of the psychodynamic psychotherapist and how to teach them in supervision. *Psychotherapy: Theory, Research, Practice, Training*, *47*(1), 20–27.

Selects from an existing list of psychotherapist competencies those that best characterize the psychodynamic psychotherapist and demonstrates, via a vignette, how one may teach those competencies in relational psychodynamic supervision.

Sarnat, J. (2012). Supervising psychoanalytic psychotherapy: Present knowledge, pressing needs, future possibilities. *Journal of Contemporary Psychotherapy*, *42*, 151–160. http://dx.doi.org/10.1007/s10879-011-9201-5

A look at the evidence for the efficacy of a relational approach to psychodynamic supervision and how supervisors may improve their supervisory technique.

Sarnat, J., & Seligman, S. (2014). Working with disruption in the supervisory relationship: Introduction to panel. *Psychoanalytic Dialogues, 24*, 523–524.

Berman, E. (2014). Psychoanalytic supervision in a heterogeneous theoretical context: Benefits and complications. *Psychoanalytic Dialogues, 24*, 525–531.

Sarnat, J. (2014). Disruption and working through in the supervisory process: A vignette from supervision of a psychoanalytic candidate. *Psychoanalytic Dialogues, 24*, 532–539.

Bass, A. (2014). Supervision and analysis at a crossroad: The development of the analytic therapist: Discussion of papers by Joan Sarnat and Emanuel Berman. *Psychoanalytic Dialogues, 24*, 540–548.

A panel on supervision that includes an introduction, two clinical papers, and a discussion, all written from a relational psychoanalytic perspective.

Slavin, J. H. (1998). Influence and vulnerability in psychoanalytic supervision and treatment. *Psychoanalytic Psychology, 15*, 230–244. http://dx.doi.org/10.1037/0736-9735.15.2.230

The implications of the shift of the role of the supervisor from someone who exercises power to someone who participates in a relationship based upon mutual vulnerability.

Szecsödy, I. (2008). Does anything go in psychoanalytic supervision? *Psychoanalytic Inquiry, 28*, 373–386. http://dx.doi.org/10.1080/07351690801962455

Concepts for studying and evaluating supervisor performance, with relational perspectives included.

Szecsödy, I., & Bornstein, M. (Eds.). (2014). Special issue: Never ever stop learning more about supervision. *Psychoanalytic Inquiry, 34*, 523–644.

An issue on psychoanalytic supervision from multiple perspectives, some of them relational.

Tummala-Narra, P. (2004). Dynamics of race and culture in the supervisory encounter. *Psychoanalytic Psychology, 21*, 300–311. http://dx.doi.org/10.1037/0736-9735.21.2.300

Writing from a relational perspective, the author asserts that the integration of cultural diversity issues in clinical supervision is an essential component of teaching competence and has important implications for addressing clients' intrapsychic and interpersonal worlds.

Watkins, C. E., Jr. (2014). The learning alliance in psychoanalytic supervision: A fifty-year retrospective and prospective. *Psychoanalytic Psychology, 32(3)*, 451–481. http://dx.doi.org/10.1037/a0034039

The history of the learning alliance, an important part of the supervisory relationship in psychoanalytic supervision, including relational updates.

Yerushalmi, H. (1999). Mutual influences in supervision. *Contemporary Psychoanalysis, 35*, 415–436.

Illustrates the pedagogical power of the supervisor relinquishing a position of authority as a conveyor of knowledge and becoming a participant in a mutual influence process.

Zicht, S. R. (2013). On the experiential and psychotherapeutic dimensions of psychoanalytic supervision: An interpersonal perspective. *American Journal of Psychoanalysis, 73*, 8–29.

A plea for supervision to be an experiential, psychotherapeutic encounter, argued from an interpersonal psychoanalytic perspective.

References

Altman, N. (1995). *The analyst in the inner city: Race, class, and culture through a psychoanalytic lens.* Hillsdale, NJ: Analytic Press.

Altman, N. (2006). Whiteness. *The Psychoanalytic Quarterly, 75,* 45–72. http://dx.doi.org/10.1002/j.2167-4086.2006.tb00032.x

American Psychological Association. (2003). Guidelines on multicultural education, training, research, practice, and organizational change for psychologists. *American Psychologist, 58,* 377–402.

American Psychological Association. (2010). *Ethical principles of psychologists and code of conduct (2002, Amended June 1, 2010).* Retrieved from http://www.apa.org/ethics/code/

American Psychological Association. (2014). *Guidelines for clinical supervision in health service psychology.* Retrieved from http://www.apa.org/about/policy/guidelines-supervision.pdf

American Psychological Association. (2015). *Relational psychodynamic psychotherapy supervision* [DVD]. Washington, DC: American Psychological Association.

Ancis, J. R., & Ladany, N. (2001). Multicultural supervision. In L. J. Bradley & N. Ladany (Eds.), *Counselor supervision: Principles, process, and practice* (3rd ed., pp. 63–90). Philadelphia, PA: Brunner-Routledge.

Ancis, J. R., & Ladany, N. (2010). A multicultural framework for counseling supervision. In N. Ladany & L. J. Bradley (Eds.), *Counselor supervision: Principles, process, and practice* (4th ed., pp. 53–95). Philadelphia, PA: Brunner-Routledge.

Aron, L. (1996). *A meeting of minds: Mutuality in psychoanalysis.* Hillsdale, NJ: Analytic Press.

Aron, L., & Bushra, A. (1998). Mutual regression: Altered states in the psychoanalytic situation. *Journal of the American Psychoanalytic Association, 46*, 389–412. http://dx.doi.org/10.1177/00030651980460020302

Aron, L., & Starr, K. (2013). *A psychotherapy for the people: Toward a progressive psychoanalysis.* New York, NY: Routledge.

Beck, J., Sarnat, J., & Barenstein, V. (2008). Psychotherapy-based approaches to supervision. In C. A. Falender & E. P. Shafranske (Eds.), *Casebook for clinical supervision: A competency-based approach* (pp. 57–96). Washington, DC: American Psychological Association. http://dx.doi.org/10.1037/11792-004

Beebe, B., & Lachmann, F. M. (1988). The contribution of mother-infant mutual influence to the origins of self and object representations. *Psychoanalytic Psychology, 5*, 305–337. http://dx.doi.org/10.1037/0736-9735.5.4.305

Bergmann, M. S. (2003). A contribution to the supervisory panel. *Psychoanalytic Dialogues, 13*, 327–339. http://dx.doi.org/10.1080/10481881309348737

Berman, E. (2004). *Impossible training: A relational view of psychoanalytic education.* Mahwah, NJ: Analytic Press.

Bernard, J. M., & Goodyear, R. L. (1998). *Fundamentals of clinical supervision* (2nd ed.). Boston, MA: Allyn & Bacon.

Bernard, J. M., & Goodyear, R. L. (2014). *Fundamentals of clinical supervision* (5th ed.). Upper Saddle River, NJ: Merrill.

Binder, J. L. (1999). Issues in teaching and learning time-limited psychodynamic psychotherapy. *Clinical Psychology Review, 19*(6), 705–719. http://dx.doi.org/10.1016/S0272-7358(98)00078-6

Binder, J. (2011, August). *Teaching and supervising psychodynamic psychotherapy.* Paper presented at the annual meeting of the American Psychological Association, Washington, DC.

Bion, W. R. (1961). *Experiences in groups.* London, UK: Tavistock. http://dx.doi.org/10.4324/9780203359075

Bion, W. R. (1962). *Learning from experience.* London, UK: Heinemann.

Black, M. J. (2003). Afterword. *Psychoanalytic Dialogues, 13*, 367–375. http://dx.doi.org/10.1080/10481881309348740

Bollas, C. (1987). *The shadow of the object: Psychoanalysis of the unthought known.* London, UK: Free Association Books.

Bordin, E. (1983). A working alliance based model of supervision. *The Counseling Psychologist, 11*, 35–42. http://dx.doi.org/10.1177/0011000083111007

Brickman, C. (2003). *Aboriginal populations in the mind: Race and primitivity in psychoanalysis.* New York, NY: Columbia University Press.

Brightman, B. K. (1984–1985). Narcissistic issues in the training experience of the psychotherapist. *International Journal of Psychoanalytic Psychotherapy, 10*, 293–317.

Buechler, S. (2013). Messages conveyed in supervision: Commentary on paper by Dana L. Castellano. *Psychoanalytic Dialogues, 23*, 733–736. http://dx.doi.org/10.1080/10481885.2013.851567

Burka, J. B., Sarnat, J. E., & St. John, C. (2007). Learning from experience in case conference: A Bionian approach to teaching and consulting. *The International Journal of Psychoanalysis, 88*, 981–1000. http://dx.doi.org/10.1516/W766-4007-8205-5478

Burkard, A. W., Johnson, A. J., Madison, M. B., Pruitt, N. T., Contreras-Tadych, D. A., Kozlowski, J. M., & Knox, S. (2006). Supervisor cultural responsiveness and unresponsiveness in cross-cultural supervision. *Journal of Counseling Psychology, 53*, 288–301.

Cabaniss, D. L. (2008). Becoming a school: Developing learning objectives for psychoanalytic education. *Psychoanalytic Inquiry, 28*, 262–277. http://dx.doi.org/10.1080/07351690801960814

Cabaniss, D. L. (2012). Teaching psychodynamics in the twenty-first century. *Journal of the American Psychoanalytic Association, 60*, 483–492. http://dx.doi.org/10.1177/0003065112446191

Cabaniss, D. L., Cherry, S., Douglas, C. J., & Schwartz, A. R. (2011). *Psychodynamic psychotherapy: A clinical manual.* West Sussex, UK: Wiley.

Castellano, D. L. (2013). Trauma triangles and parallel processes: Geometry and the supervisor/trainee/patient triad. *Psychoanalytic Dialogues, 23*, 720–732. http://dx.doi.org/10.1080/10481885.2013.851566

Chang, S. (2015, April). *Panel: Sex, love, and kinship in the twenty-first century.* Division of Psychoanalysis (39) Spring Meeting, San Francisco, CA.

Cooper, L., & Gustafson, J. P. (1985). Supervision in a group: An application of group theory. *The Clinical Supervisor, 3*, 7–25. http://dx.doi.org/10.1300/J001v03n02_02

Crits-Christoph, P., Connelly Gibbons, M. B., & Mukherjee, D. (2013). Psychotherapy process-outcome research. In M. J. Lambert (Ed.), *Handbook of psychotherapy and behavior change* (6th ed., pp. 298–339). Hoboken, NJ: John Wiley and Sons, Inc.

Cushman, P. (2000). White guilt, political activity, and the analyst: Commentary on paper by Neil Altman. *Psychoanalytic Dialogues, 10*, 607–618. http://dx.doi.org/10.1080/10481881009348570

Dalal, F. (2006). Racism: Processes of detachment, dehumanization, and hatred. *The Psychoanalytic Quarterly, 75*, 131–161. http://dx.doi.org/10.1002/j.2167-4086.2006.tb00035.x

Davies, J. M., & Frawley, M. G. (1994). *Treating the adult survivor of childhood sexual abuse: A psychoanalytic perspective.* New York, NY: Basic Books.

DeBell, D. (1981). Supervisory styles and positions. In R. Wallerstein (Ed.), *Becoming a psychotherapist* (pp. 39–60). New York, NY: International Universities Press.

Dent, V. (2007). Three's a crowd: One patient, multiple practitioners, and the problem of splitting. *Psychoanalytic Psychotherapy, 24,* 157–174.

Dewald, P. (1987). *Learning process in psychoanalytic supervision: Complexities and challenges.* Madison, CT: International Universities Press.

Divino, C., & Moore, M. S. (2010). Integrating neurobiological findings into psychodynamic psychotherapy training and practice. *Psychoanalytic Dialogues, 20,* 337–355. http://dx.doi.org/10.1080/10481885.2010.481613

Doehrman, M. J. (1976). Parallel processes in supervision and psychotherapy. *Bulletin of the Menninger Clinic, 40,* 9–104.

Ebbert, N. (2011, May). *Learning from experience together: Perils and pleasures of collaborative supervision.* Paper presented at the Psychotherapy Institute Supervisors' Conclave, Oakland, CA.

Eckler-Hart, A. H. (1987). True and false self in the development of the psychotherapist. *Psychotherapy: Theory, Research, Practice, Training, 24,* 683–692.

Eizirik, C. L. (2014). Discussion (II): Never ever stop learning more about supervision. *Psychoanalytic Inquiry, 34,* 642–643. http://dx.doi.org/10.1080/07351690.2014.924376

Ekstein, R., & Wallerstein, R. (1972). *The teaching and learning of psychotherapy* (2nd ed.). New York, NY: International Universities Press.

Elkind, S. N. (1992). *Resolving impasses in therapeutic relationships.* New York, NY: Guilford Press.

Ellis, M. V., & Ladany, N. (1997). Inferences concerning supervisees and clients in clinical supervision: An integrative review. In C. E. Watkins, Jr., (Ed.), *Handbook of psychotherapy supervision* (pp. 467–507). New York, NY: Wiley.

Eng, D. L., & Han, S. A. (2000). A dialogue on racial melancholia. *Psychoanalytic Dialogues, 10,* 667–700. http://dx.doi.org/10.1080/10481881009348576

Falender, C. A., & Shafranske, E. P. (2004). *Clinical supervision: A competency-based approach.* Washington, DC: American Psychological Association. http://dx.doi.org/10.1037/10806-000

Fleming, J., & Benedek, T. F. (1966). *Psychoanalytic supervision.* New York, NY: Grune & Stratton.

Frawley-O'Dea, M. G. (1997a). Supervision amidst abuse: The supervisee's perspective. In M. H. Rock (Ed.), *Psychodynamic supervision* (pp. 312–335). Northvale, NJ: Jason Aronson.

Frawley-O'Dea, M. G. (1997b). Who's doing what to whom? Supervision and sexual abuse. *Contemporary Psychoanalysis, 33*, 5–18. http://dx.doi.org/10.1080/00107530.1997.10746966

Frawley-O'Dea, M. G. (1997c, February). *Supervision in the second century: A relational model of supervision.* Paper presented at the 17th annual spring meeting of the Division of Psychoanalysis (39) of the American Psychological Association, Denver, CO.

Frawley-O'Dea, M. G. (1998). Revisiting the "teach/treat" boundary in psychoanalytic supervision: When the supervisee is or is not in concurrent treatment. *The Journal of the American Academy of Psychoanalysis, 26*, 513–527.

Frawley-O'Dea, M. G. (2003). Supervision is a relationship too: A contemporary approach to psychoanalytic supervision. Symposium on psychoanalytic training and education. *Psychoanalytic Dialogues, 13*, 355–366. http://dx.doi.org/10.1080/10481881309348739

Frawley-O'Dea, M. G., & Sarnat, J. (2001). *The supervisory relationship: A contemporary psychodynamic approach.* New York, NY: Guilford Press.

Gay, P. (1988). *Freud.* New York, NY: Doubleday.

Gediman, H. K., & Wolkenfeld, F. (1980). The parallelism phenomenon in psychoanalysis and supervision: Its reconsideration as a triadic system. *The Psychoanalytic Quarterly, 49*, 234–255.

Goren, E. (2013). Ethics, boundaries, and supervision: Commentary on "Trauma triangles and parallel processes: Geometry and the supervisor/trainee/patient triad." *Psychoanalytic Dialogues, 23*, 737–743. http://dx.doi.org/10.1080/10481885.2013.851568

Grant, J., Schofield, M. J., & Crawford, S. (2012). Managing difficulties in supervision: Supervisors' perspectives. *Journal of Counseling Psychology, 59*, 528–541. http://dx.doi.org/10.1037/a0030000

Gray, L. A., Ladany, N., Walker, J. A., & Ancis, J. R. (2001). Psychotherapy trainees' experience of counterproductive events in supervision. *Journal of Counseling Psychology, 48*, 371–383.

Gurevich, H. (2008). The language of absence. *The International Journal of Psychoanalysis, 89*, 561–578. http://dx.doi.org/10.1111/j.1745-8315.2008.00056.x

Hamer, F. M. (2006). Racism as a transference state: Episodes of racial hostility in the psychoanalytic context. *The Psychoanalytic Quarterly, 75*, 197–214. http://dx.doi.org/10.1002/j.2167-4086.2006.tb00037.x

Hassinger, J. A. (2014). Twenty-first-century living color: Racialized enactment in psychoanalysis. *Psychoanalysis, Culture & Society, 19*, 337–359. http://dx.doi.org/10.1057/pcs.2014.39

Hirsch, I. (1997). Supervision amidst abuse: The supervisor's perspective. In M. H. Rock (Ed.), *Psychodynamic supervision* (pp. 339–360). Northvale, NJ: Jason Aronson.

Hirsch, I. (1998). Discussion of Frawley-O'Dea and Sarnat: Emotional and interactional factors in the supervisory relationship. *The Journal of the American Academy of Psychoanalysis, 26*, 545–552.

Jarmon, H. (1990). The supervisory experience: An object relations perspective. *Psychotherapy: Theory, Research, Practice, Training, 22*, 195–201.

Josephs, L. (1990). The concrete attitude and the supervision of beginning psychotherapy. *Psychoanalytic Psychotherapy, 8*(1), 11–22.

Kaslow, N. J., Borden, K. A., Collins, F. L., Forrest, L., Illfelder-Kaye, J., Nelson, P. D., et al. (2004). Competencies Conference: Future directions in education and credentialing in professional psychology. *Journal of Clinical Psychology, 80*, 699–712.

Kernberg, O. F. (2010). Psychoanalytic supervision: The supervisor's tasks. *The Psychoanalytic Quarterly, 79*, 603–627. http://dx.doi.org/10.1002/j.2167-4086.2010. tb00459.x

Kris, E. (1936). The psychology of caricature. *The International Journal of Psychoanalysis, 17*, 285–303.

Lachmann, F. M. (2001). Some contributions of empirical infant research to adult psychoanalysis. *Psychoanalytic Dialogues, 11*, 167–185. http://dx.doi.org/ 10.1080/10481881109348605

Ladany, N., & Bradley, L. (2010). *Counselor supervision* (4th ed.). New York, NY: Routledge.

Ladany, N., Friedlander, M. L., & Nelson, M. L. (2005). *Critical events in psychotherapy supervision: An interpersonal approach.* Washington, DC: American Psychological Association. http://dx.doi.org/10.1037/10958-000

Ladany, N., Hill, C., Corbett, M., & Nutt, E. (1996). Nature, extent, and importance of what psychotherapy trainees do not disclose to their supervisors. *Journal of Counseling Psychology, 43*, 10–24. http://dx.doi.org/10.1037/0022-0167.43.1.10

Ladany, N., & Lehrman-Waterman, D. E. (1999). The content and frequency of supervisor self-disclosures and their relationship to supervisor style and supervisory working alliance. *Counselor Education and Supervision, 38*, 143–160. http://dx.doi.org/10.1002/j.1556-6978.1999.tb00567.x

Ladany, N., & Walker, J. A. (2003). Supervisor self-disclosure: Balancing the uncontrollable narcissist with the indomitable altruist. *Journal of Clinical Psychology, 59*, 611–621. http://dx.doi.org/10.1002/jclp.10164

Layton, L. (2006). Racial identities, racial enactments, and normative unconscious processes. *The Psychoanalytic Quarterly, 75*, 237–269. http://dx.doi. org/10.1002/j.2167-4086.2006.tb00039.x

Leary, K. (2000). Racial enactments in dynamic treatment. *Psychoanalytic Dialogues, 10*, 639–653. http://dx.doi.org/10.1080/10481881009348573

Mayer, E. L. (1996). Changes in science and changing ideas about knowledge and authority in psychoanalysis. *The Psychoanalytic Quarterly, 65*, 158–200.

Moga, D. E., & Cabaniss, D. L. (2014). Learning objectives for supervision: Benefits for candidates and beyond. *Psychoanalytic Inquiry, 34*, 528–537. http://dx.doi.org/10.1080/07351690.2014.924367

Moskowitz, S. A., & Rupert, P. A. (1983). Conflict resolution within the supervisory relationship. *Professional Psychology: Research and Practice, 14*, 632–641. http://dx.doi.org/10.1037/0735-7028.14.5.632

Nagell, N., Steinmetzer, L., Fissabre, U., & Spilski, J. (2014). Research into the relationship experience in supervision and its influence on the psychoanalytical identity formation of candidate trainees. *Psychoanalytic Inquiry, 34*, 554–583. http://dx.doi.org/10.1080/07351690.2014.924370

Nelson, M. L., Barnes, K. L., Evans, A. L., & Triggiano, P. J. (2008). Working with conflict in clinical supervision: Wise supervisors' perspectives. *Journal of Counseling Psychology, 55*, 172–184. http://dx.doi.org/10.1037/0022-0167.55.2.172

Ogden, T. H. (1994). *Subjects of analysis.* Northvale, NJ: Jason Aronson.

Ogden, T. H. (2003). On not being able to dream. *The International Journal of Psychoanalysis, 84*, 17–30. http://dx.doi.org/10.1516/1D1W-025P-10VJ-TMRW

Ogden, T. H. (2005). On psychoanalytic supervision. *The International Journal of Psychoanalysis, 86*, 1265–1280. http://dx.doi.org/10.1516/BEE8-C9E7-J7Q7-24BF

Orlinsky, D., Grawe, K., & Parks, B. (1994). Process and outcome in psychotherapy. In A. D. Bergin & S. L. Garfield (Eds.), *Handbook of psychotherapy and behavior change* (4th ed., pp. 270–376). New York, NY: Wiley.

Racker, H. (1957). The meanings and uses of countertransference. *The Psychoanalytic Quarterly, 26*, 303–357.

Raubolt, R. (2006). *Power games: Influence, persuasion, and indoctrination in psychotherapy training.* New York, NY: Other Press.

Riggs, S. A., & Bretz, K. M. (2006). Attachment processes in the supervisory relationship: An exploratory investigation. *Professional Psychology: Research and Practice, 37*, 558–566. http://dx.doi.org/10.1037/0735-7028.37.5.558

Rønnestad, M. H., & Skovholt, T. M. (2003). The journey of the counselor and therapist: Research findings and perspectives on professional development. *Journal of Career Development, 30*, 5–44. http://dx.doi.org/10.1177/089484530303000102

Rønnestad, M. H., & Skovholt, T. M. (2013). *The developing practitioner: Growth and stagnation of therapists and counselors.* New York, NY: Routledge.

Safran, J. D., & Muran, J. C. (2000). *Negotiating the therapeutic alliance: A relational treatment guide.* New York, NY: Guilford Press.

Sarnat, J. (1992). Supervision in relationship: Resolving the teach/treat dilemma in psychoanalytic supervision. *Psychoanalytic Psychology, 9,* 387–403.

Sarnat, J. (1997). The contribution of a process-oriented case conference to the development of students in the first year of a doctor of psychology program. *The Clinical Supervisor, 15*(2), 163–180. http://dx.doi.org/10.1300/J001v15n02_12

Sarnat, J. E. (1998). Rethinking the role of regressive experience in psychoanalytic supervision. *The Journal of the American Academy of Psychoanalysis, 26,* 529–543.

Sarnat, J. (2006). Authority relations in psychodynamic supervision: A contemporary view. In R. Raubolt (Ed.), *Power games: Influence, persuasion, and indoctrination in psychotherapy training* (pp. 255–271). New York, NY: Other Press.

Sarnat, J. (2008). Reuniting the psychic couple in analytic training and practice: A candidate's experience. *Psychoanalytic Psychology, 25,* 110–121. http://dx.doi.org/10.1037/0736-9735.25.1.110

Sarnat, J. (2010). Key competencies of the psychodynamic psychotherapist and how to teach them in supervision. *Psychotherapy: Theory, Research, Practice, Training, 47*(1), 20–27.

Sarnat, J. (2012). Supervising psychoanalytic psychotherapy: Present knowledge, pressing needs, future possibilities. *Journal of Contemporary Psychotherapy, 42,* 151–160. http://dx.doi.org/10.1007/s10879-011-9201-5

Sarnat, J. (2014). Disruption and working through in the supervisory process: A vignette from *Supervision of a psychoanalytic candidate. Psychoanalytic Dialogues, 24,* 532–539. http://dx.doi.org/10.1080/10481885.2014.949486

Schore, A. (2011). The right brain implicit self lies at the core of psychoanalysis. *Psychoanalytic Dialogues, 21,* 75–100. http://dx.doi.org/10.1080/10481885.2011.545329

Silverman, D. (2005). What works in psychotherapy and how do we know? What evidence-based practice has to offer. *Psychoanalytic Psychology, 22,* 306–312. http://dx.doi.org/10.1037/0736-9735.22.2.306

Slavin, J. H. (1998). Influence and vulnerability in psychoanalytic supervision and treatment. *Psychoanalytic Psychology, 15,* 230–244. http://dx.doi.org/10.1037/0736-9735.15.2.230

Stern, D. B. (1997). *Unformulated experience: From dissociation to imagination in psychoanalysis.* Hillsdale, NJ: Analytic Press.

Stern, D. N. (1985). *The interpersonal world of the infant.* New York, NY: Basic Books.

Strupp, H. H., & Anderson, T. (1997). On the limitations of therapy manuals. *Clinical Psychology: Science and Practice, 4,* 76–82. http://dx.doi.org/10.1111/j.1468-2850.1997.tb00101.x

Strupp, H. H., & Binder, J. (1984). *Psychotherapy in a new key: A guide to time-limited dynamic psychotherapy.* New York, NY: Basic Books.

Suchet, M. (2007). Unraveling whiteness. *Psychoanalytic Dialogues, 17,* 867–886. http://dx.doi.org/10.1080/10481880701703730

Szecsödy, I. (1990). *The learning process in psychotherapy supervision* (Doctoral dissertation). Stockholm, Sweden: Karolinska Institutet.

Szecsödy, I. (2008). Does anything go in psychoanalytic supervision? *Psychoanalytic Inquiry, 28,* 373–386. http://dx.doi.org/10.1080/07351690801962455

Szecsödy, I. (2012). More research is essential on how to increase competence in supervision and supervision training. *Nordic Psychology, 64,* 218–226. http://dx.doi.org/10.1080/19012276.2012.731315

Szecsödy, I. (2013). Supervision should be a mutual learning experience. *The Scandinavian Psychoanalytic Review, 36,* 119–129.

Szönyi, G. (2014). The vicissitudes of the Budapest model of supervision: Can we learn from it today? *Psychoanalytic Inquiry, 34,* 606–618. http://dx.doi.org/10.1080/07351690.2014.924373

Thomas, J. T. (2010). *The ethics of supervision and consultation.* Washington, DC: American Psychological Association.

Tuckett, D. (2005). Does anything go? Towards a framework for the more transparent assessment of psychoanalytic competence. *The International Journal of Psychoanalysis, 86,* 31–49. http://dx.doi.org/10.1516/R2U5-XJ37-7DFJ-DD18

Tummala-Narra, P. (2004). Dynamics of race and culture in the supervisory encounter. *Psychoanalytic Psychology, 21,* 300–311. http://dx.doi.org/10.1037/0736-9735.21.2.300

Tummala-Narra, P. (2015). Cultural competence as a core emphasis of psychoanalytic psychotherapy. *Psychoanalytic Psychology, 32,* 275–292. http://dx.doi.org/10.1037/a0034041

Ulmer, N. (2011). *Contemplating supervision: A neuropsychoanalytic relational perspective. Lecture for the Supervision Study Program.* Berkeley, CA: The Psychotherapy Institute.

Ungar, V. R., & de Ahumada, L. B. (2001). Supervision: A container-contained approach. *The International Journal of Psychoanalysis, 82,* 71–81. http://dx.doi.org/10.1516/LUM2-4C9E-PE5C-V88Y

Vivona, J. M. (2006). From developmental metaphor to developmental model: The shrinking role of language in the talking cure. *Journal of the American Psychoanalytic Association, 54,* 877–901. http://dx.doi.org/10.1177/00030651060540031501

Walt, A., & Slome, L. (2015). Black analysts speak. *The Psychoanalytic Institute of Northern California News & Notes, 23,* 16.

Watkins, C. E., Jr. (Ed.) (1997). *Handbook of psychotherapy supervision*. New York, NY: Wiley.

Watkins, C. E., Jr. (2010). Psychoanalytic constructs. *American Journal of Psychotherapy, 64*, 393–416.

Watkins, C. E., Jr. (2011). Celebrating psychoanalytic supervision: Considering a century of seminal contribution. *Psychoanalytic Review, 98*, 401–418. http://dx.doi.org/10.1521/prev.2011.98.3.401

Watkins, C. E., Jr. (2013). Psychoanalytic supervision in the new millennium: On pressing needs and impressing possibilities. *International Forum of Psychoanalysis.* http://dx.doi.org/10.1080/0803706X.2013.779748

Watkins, C. E., Jr. (2014). On psychoanalytic supervision as signature pedagogy. *Psychoanalytic Review, 101*, 175–195.

Watkins, C. E., Jr. (2015). Toward a research-informed, evidence-based psychoanalytic supervision. *Psychoanalytic Psychotherapy, 29*, 5–19. http://dx.doi.org/10.1080/02668734.2014.980305

Welfare, L. (2010). Evaluation in supervision. In N. Ladany & L. Bradley (Eds.), *Counselor supervision* (4th ed.; pp. 357–352). New York, NY: Routledge.

Whiston, S. C., & Emerson, S. (1989). Ethical implications for supervisors in counseling of trainees. *Counselor Education and Supervision, 28*, 318–325. http://dx.doi.org/10.1002/j.1556-6978.1989.tb01122.x

Yourman, D. B., & Farber, B. A. (1996). Nondisclosure of distortion in psychotherapy supervision. *Psychotherapy: Theory, Research, Practice, Training, 33*, 567–575.

Index

Notes. *See also* Process notes
  by supervisor and supervisee,
    60–61
  for supervisor's personal use, 60
Novice psychotherapists, 133–134

Objective expert, supervisor as, 130
Objectivity, 11
One-person, intrapsychic models, 8
Openness to processing conflict, in
    supervision, 37
Outcome evaluation, 102

Parental couple, 85
Partnership between supervisor and
    supervisee: valuing methods
    that contribute, 48
Patient
  "channeling" of by supervisee, 41
  psychology of, 20
  supervisee difficulties impact on,
    96–98
  transference of, 40–41
Personal crisis, supervisee in, 93–94
Personal development, supervisor-
    focused 102, 103
Personal disclosure, 37–38, 58–59,
    116–118, 146n5
Personal use, notes for, 60
Politicization, of supervision, 7
Possibilities for future growth in
    supervision
  experiential learning, 133–134
  routine supervisory consultation,
    136–137
  supervisor education, 135–137
  team approaches to supervising,
    137
Power
  abuse of, 126–127
  mutuality of authority and, 77–78
Power differential, in supervisory
    relationships, 37

Power Games (Raubolt), 127
Power struggle, during supervisory
    hour, 76
Predoctoral psychology supervisee,
    Jane as, 3
Presenting clinical material. *See* Form
    of clinical presentation in
    supervision
Pre-session supervisor-initiated
    enactment, 82–83
Procedural knowledge transmission,
    39–40
Process
  teaching and "treating" part of a
    complex 13–14, 24
Process-consistent supervision, 6, 9,
    10
Process-inconsistent supervision, 9, 10
Process notes
  for intermediate-level and
    advanced supervisors, 57
  teaching how to write, 57–58, 132
Psychoanalysis, 7. *See also* Relational
    psychoanalysis, working with
    difference and
Psychoanalytic Dialogues, 18
Psychoanalytic learning, 66–67
Psychoanalytic research, 138
Psychoanalytic supervision
  classical model of, 18
  nonrelational approach to, 9
  relational model of, 18
Psychoanalytic theory, 8
Psychoanalytic training
  Budapest Model of, 30–31
  of Frawley-O'Dea, 9, 10
Psychodynamic psychotherapists,
    41–42
Psychodynamic psychotherapy
  psychoanalysis and, 7
  relational model of, 7–8
Psychodynamic psychotherapy
  supervision, 11. *See also*

Relational psychodynamic case
  conference
  Bion's theory of groups, relational
    case conference leader and,
    62–64
  vignette of, 64–65
*Relational Psychodynamic Psycho-
  therapy Supervision*, 69
Relational supervisor
  clinical expertise of, 24, 26
  functions of, 31
  working with inappropriate
    supervisee behavior,
    122–126
  working with supervisee's
    transferential feelings,
    26–27
Relationships. *See also* Jane, Susie's
    relationship with; Supervisory
    relationships
  clinical, 4, 48
  difficulties with, 71–72, 73,
    75–76
  focus on, 20–21
  Frawley-O'Dea on, 20
  frustration with, 71, 75, 77, 78
  growth-promoting, 12
  loss in, 79, 80, 84
  power differential in, 37
Research
  expansion of, 137–138
  about supervision, ix, 5–6
Research literature. *See also* Education
    and cognitive research
    literature; Neuroscience
    research literature; Psycho-
    analytic supervision research
    literature
  for counseling psychology, 35–38
  on psychodynamic psychotherapy,
    38–39
Responsibilities, of supervision, ix
Rønnestad, M. H., ix, 51–52, 54, 89

Sarah
  difficulties of, 96–98
  intervention with, 96–98
  regression of, 97
Schore, A., 42–43
Self-awareness. *See* Supervisor self-
  awareness
Self-supervision, 108
Separation anxiety, 85
Sexual encounters and boundaries, 116
Shifts, in supervisory relationship, 78–82
Skills
  complex, 40–41
  interpersonal, 40
  for working with difference, 102
Skovholt, T. M., 51–52, 54, 89
Starr, K., 7–8, 105–106
Strong feelings, evoked by supervisor's
  mode of participation, 24
Suchet, M.
  countertransference work of,
    110–112
  opening conversation on race,
    108–110
Supervised therapy, 70–71
Supervisee. *See also* Inappropriate
    supervisee behavior
  evaluation of, 59
  informed consent of, 114–115
  injury of, 82
  Jane as, 69–70
  in personal crisis, 93–94
  intermediate-level, 52–53
  personal disclosure of, 58–59, 146n5
  termination of, 96
  transferential feelings of, 26–27
  workable personality problem of,
    69–70
Supervisee difficulties
  Concluding discussion of, 100
  continuum of degree of, 90
  intrapsychic component of, 89–90
  moderate, 93–95

About the Author

Joan E. Sarnat, PhD, ABPP, is a clinical psychologist and psychoanalyst in private practice in Berkeley, California. She is Board Certified in Clinical Psychology by the American Board of Professional Psychology. She is a member of the American Psychological Association, The National Register, The International Association for Relational Psychotherapy and Psychoanalysis, and The International Psychoanalytic Association.

Dr. Sarnat is a personal and supervising analyst and member of the faculty at the Psychoanalytic Institute of Northern California, San Francisco, a theoretically pluralistic, independent, psychoanalytic institute. She has served as adjunct faculty at Antioch/New England Graduate School of Professional Psychology, Keene, New Hampshire; The University of Massachusetts, Amherst Department of Clinical Psychology; The Smith School for Social Work, Northampton, Massachusetts; Alliant University, San Francisco, California; and The University of California Extension Program, Berkeley; and established a process-oriented case conference sequence at the Wright Institute in Berkeley, California. She has supervised, led case conferences, and run consultation groups for supervisors for almost 40 years. Dr. Sarnat has lectured widely on psychoanalytic supervision and has published in numerous journals, including *Psychoanalytic Psychology*; *Psychotherapy: Theory, Research, Practice, Training*; *Psychoanalytic Dialogues*; and *The International Journal of Psychoanalysis*. She coauthored with Mary Gail Frawley-O'Dea *The Supervisory Relationship: A Contemporary Psychodynamic Approach* (2001).

In 1970, Dr. Sarnat graduated in Social Relations from Harvard College, where she studied with Erik Erikson, Jerome Kagan, and Daniel Goleman. In 1975, she received her PhD in psychology from the University of Michigan, where Edward Bordin was her primary supervisor. She completed a postdoctoral fellow at the Mount Zion Department of Psychiatry in 1978, and received a Certificate in Psychoanalysis from the Psychoanalytic Institute of Northern California in 2002.

Dr. Sarnat lives with her mathematician husband, David Hoffman, in Berkeley, California. They frequently visit their two sons, daughter-in-law, and granddaughter in Brooklyn, New York.